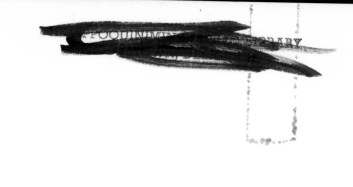

MIDDLESEX

(*overleaf*) Gentleman's Row, Enfield

BRUCE STEVENSON

MIDDLESEX

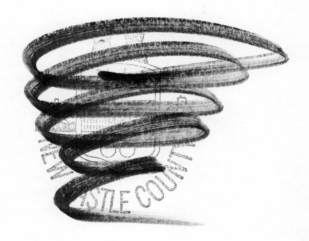

B. T. Batsford Ltd
London

to Eva

First printed 1972

© Bruce Stevenson 1972

Text printed in Great Britain by Northumberland
Press Ltd, Gateshead, Co. Durham. Plates printed and
books bound by Richard Clay (The Chaucer Press)
Ltd, Bungay, Suffolk, for the publishers B. T. Batsford
Ltd, 4 Fitzhardinge Street, London W.1

ISBN 0 7134 0070 6

CONTENTS

LIST OF ILLUSTRATIONS

ACKNOWLEDGMENTS AND BOOKS

Middlesex as a county has been very fully documented. The Royal Commission on Historical Monuments published their inventory of the county in 1937: it includes all historical monuments up to 1714. Three volumes of the *Victoria County History* have been published, with two more to come. The English Place Name Society published their volume on Middlesex in 1942. C. E. Vulliamy's *Archaeology of London and Middlesex* (1930) is of value: Sir Montagu Sharp's *Middlesex in British Roman and Saxon Times* (1932) contains much information, but also some speculation. There have been histories and surveys of the county from Norden's *Speculum Britanniae* (1593) until well into the present century. Of them only a few need be mentioned. James Thorne's *Handbook to the Environs of London* (1876) is admirable and there is much of interest in E. Walford's *Greater London* (1882-4). Sir Clifford Radcliffe's *Middlesex* (1939) is admirable in its survey of county administration. Arthur Mee's *Middlesex: Little Home County* (1940) is readable but often accepts legend for fact. Norman G. Brett-James' *Middlesex* (1951) is well planned, full of information, but marred by an inadequate index.

The essential book on the county is Michael Robbins *Middlesex* (1953), superbly organised, comprehensive and a product of deep research and even though many changes have taken place since it was written, it remains the best book on the county as a whole. Essential too for the student of architecture is Nikolaus Pevsner's *Middlesex* (1951) in the *Buildings of England* series. Equally percipient on modern developments, though not specifically on Middlesex, are two books by Ian Nairn: Nairn's *London* (1966) and *Modern Buildings in London* (1964), both of them full of brilliant observation and informed enthusiasm.

I owe thanks to many people who have provided me with information. Firstly to reference librarians (many of them merely voices on the telephone) who have been courteous, exact and expeditious. I have to thank also S. J. Butcher, librarian of Barnet for information about Hendon: J. T. Gillett (formerly librarian of Brent) for access to his unpublished history of Willesden; and Malcolm Binns, librarian of Earling for information about his borough. To my former colleague W. G. Campbell, reference librarian of Hornsey, I owe much; he has invariably supplied me with the correct answers to innumerable questions. James Page has supplied information about Hampstead Garden Suburb; Dennis Emerson about aviation; Philip Allen about canals and powder-mills.

To Samuel Carr and Mary Scriven go my thanks for their encouragement and their forbearance in delays. Lastly I owe thanks to Montague Sinclair, my companion on numberless journeys through Middlesex; without his help this survey would have taken three times as long to compile.

The Author and publishers would like to thank the following for permission to use photographs: J. Allen Cash, 29; A. F. Kersting, *frontispiece*, 2-13, 15, 18-26, 28; Popperfoto, 14, 16, 17, 27.

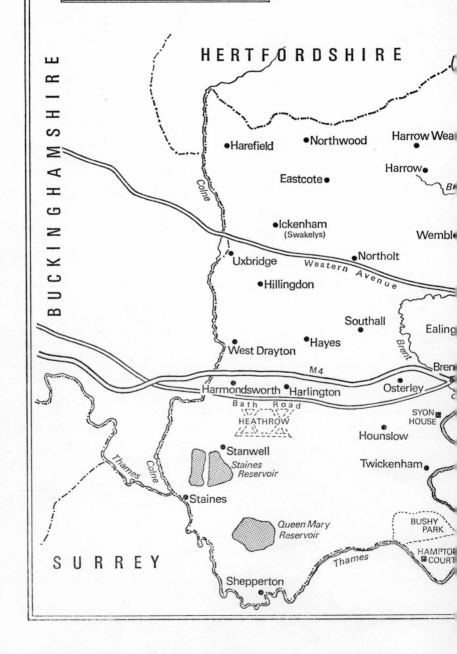

MIDDLESEX

HERTFORDSHIRE

BUCKINGHAMSHIRE

Harefield

Northwood

Harrow Wea...

Harrow

Eastcote

B...

Colne

Ickenham
(Swakelys)

Wembl...

Uxbridge

Northolt

Western Avenue

Hillingdon

Southall

Ealing

Hayes

Brent

West Drayton

M 4

Bren...

Harmondsworth Harlington

Osterley

Bath Road

SYON
HOUSE

HEATHROW

Hounslow

Stanwell

Staines
Reservoir

Twickenham

Thames

Colne

Queen Mary
Reservoir

BUSHY
PARK

Staines

HAMPTO...
COURT

Thames

SURREY

Shepperton

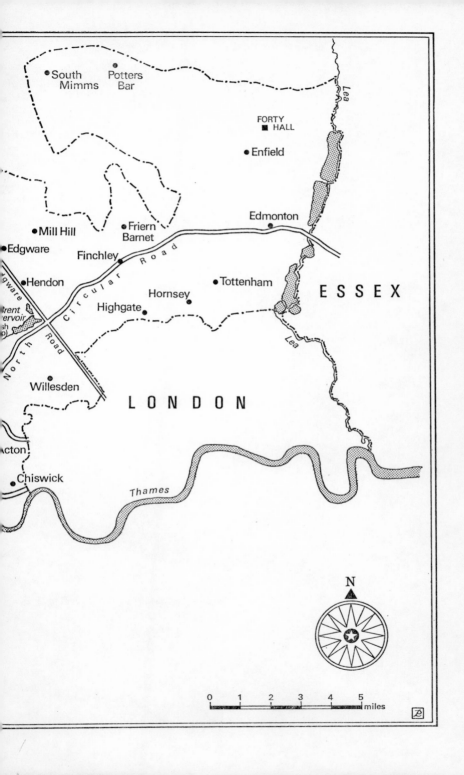

South Mimms

Potters Bar

FORTY HALL

Enfield

Edmonton

Mill Hill

Friern Barnet

Edgware

Finchley

North Circular Road

Hendon

Tottenham

Hornsey

Highgate

Brent Reservoir

ESSEX

Lea

Lea

LONDON

Willesden

Acton

Chiswick

Thames

N

0 1 2 3 4 5 miles

CHAPTER ONE

The Vanishing County

There is no doubt that Roman armies marched through Middlesex in 54 B.C., though at that time the place had not even a name. There are evidences of Roman occupation, notably in the camps at Staines and Brockley Hill, and there was in all probability a crossing of the Thames at Brentford. The three great Roman roads of Middlesex were Ermine Street (the old road to Hertford), Watling Street (the Edgware Road) and Thamesis Street (roughly corresponding to the Bath Road). It is not until A.D. 704 that the name 'Middleseaxan' appears, and the historians generally agree that this was the country of the Middle Saxons, distinguished from the country of the East Saxons in Essex, and the colonies established on the middle Thames. There are many remains of Saxon earthworks in the county, the greatest of these being Grimsdyke in Harrow : but traces of moats and camps abound, and many place-names have a Saxon origin.

At the time of the Norman conquest, Middlesex was mostly pasture and arable land, with large areas of forest : Domesday Book divided Middlesex into six 'hundreds' : Edmonton, Gore, Ossulstone, Elthorne, Hounslow and Spelthorne—these divisions had still some importance until the end of the nineteenth century, and are still in use as parliamentary and sessional divisions. In Norman times the church was the main landowner, the chief holders being the Bishop of London and the Abbot of Westminster. The major secular landowners were Geoffrey de Mandeville and the Earl of Arundel : and the names of all of them are still to be found in many parts of the county in place and street names.

There are a number of connections with English history, from the Battle of Barnet in 1471 onwards. Henry VIII was the owner of a number of manors in Middlesex. Elizabeth I lived as a princess at Enfield, and her progresses through the county are recorded in the history of such great houses as Harefield and Osterley. Middlesex men played a part in the Babington plot of 1586, and Gunpowder plot in 1605. The Civil War surged round Brentford and Turnham Green in 1642, and its treaty negotiations were held in Uxbridge. The Parliamentary generals, especially, had their homes in Middlesex, and in the eighteenth and nineteenth century the county was rich in literary and political associations.

Middlesex, however, has always been dominated by London. It was still countryside in the seventeenth century, when many prosperous merchants and bankers moved there to build their fine houses. The land was largely agricultural and market gardening, with many orchards, the produce going to the metropolis. Milling and other small industries grew up round the rivers: the Thames, the Colne and the Lea. The chief industry was brickmaking in the plain extending from Brentford to West Drayton: a number of the great houses in the county, including Hampton Court Palace, were built of Middlesex bricks. Allied to this industry is the dredging of gravel: rights for this were first granted in 1636. The industry continues to the present day, with over three million cubic yards of gravel taken out every year. To brickmaking and gravel-taking can be ascribed the bleakness of the Middlesex plain, evident even in 1830 to Cobbett when he wrote of Middlesex as 'bad in soil and villainous in look'. Transport of goods in the county was until the nineteenth century chiefly by river and canal, though most of the roads had been turnpiked by 1720. It was only with the advent of macadamisation in 1830 that road communications became good: but there were still complaints about the country lanes which honeycombed Middlesex until the end of the nineteenth century. The turnpike age, however, gave the county some fine coaching inns, many of which are still preserved.

It was the Railway Age that transformed Middlesex from countryside into what it is today. As the railways pushed out of London, so settlement after settlement grew up around branch stations. The proliferation of branch lines, their subsequent electrification, and the advent of London Transport completed the transformation: the county became a series of suburbs. The development of arterial roads and motorways has made further and more ruthless changes in the Middlesex landscape.

Enormous changes have taken place in the government of the county in the last 80 years. Before 1889 the county of Middlesex comprised the whole of London north of the Thames, with the exception of the City of London. After 1889 the passing of the Local Government Act meant that a large part of the population disappeared with the formation of the county of London and the metropolitan boroughs. The districts administered by the new Middlesex County Council were all 'Urban Districts'. It was only in the twentieth century that some of these districts grew large enough and wealthy enough to become boroughs in their own right, the first being Ealing in 1901. The County Council had the power to levy rates: it administered justice, education, roads and public health, and many other powers were added during this century.

In 1965, the London Boroughs Act came into operation, and Middlesex as a County administrative area went out of existence. Instead nine 'London Boroughs' were formed by a series of amalgamations: they were Barnet, Brent, Ealing, Haringey, Harrow, Hillingdon, Hounslow and Richmond-upon-Thames. There were adjustments of boundaries: Potters Bar became part of Hertfordshire: Staines and Sunbury were taken into the County of Surrey. Although the Middlesex County Council is a thing of the past, the county itself still exists as an entity, and its inhabitants still think of themselves as 'living' in Middlesex. There has indeed been no pride of county, such as is found in Kent or Sussex. In 40 years residence I have never met 'a man of Middlesex' or heard anything that could be called a Middlesex accent. There are vestiges of loyalty to the name, especially among army men. Many now living have been proud to belong to the 'Die-Hards', thus named after their conduct at the Battle of Albuera in 1811. But the 57th Foot of 1782, known as the Middlesex Regiment, is now disbanded, its drill-halls empty, its records in store. There are loyalties, too, to the Middlesex Cricket Club, though their headquarters have always been inside London. Even the County Administrative headquarters have never been inside the County boundaries, but in Westminster. There have been four Middlesex Guildhalls, the last of them opened in 1913. Today the Guildhall in Parliament Square is a court house only, though it still houses a notable collection of portraits of Middlesex worthies. The fine collection of archives in the County Record Office has now been taken over by the Greater London Council. So Middlesex exists as a name, a number of loyalties, and a postal address: though as a county it may be said to be vanishing.

Middlesex, the second smallest county in area is at the same time the most urbanised, with a population of nearly 2,250,000 in 1968. Densely populated in the areas nearest to the metropolis, in Edmonton, Tottenham, Hornsey and Willesden, the houses thin out in the northern areas, with much land in London's green belt. Rural areas remain along the borders with Buckinghamshire, and overall there are still 10,000 acres of preserved open space. From another point of view the county is a vast collection of suburbs, large and small, each with its churches and chapels, schools, great areas of housing and shopping centres. There are also concentrations of factories, some planned, like Park Royal, others along the great arterial roads. Zoning of factories has been the rule in the last 30 years, but there are still hundreds of older factories placed seemingly at random in every borough of Middlesex. To these must be added the large number of tremendous office buildings erected during the last ten years. Middlesex is constantly changing: and the tendency is towards uniformity. John Betjeman in his *Victorian and Edwardian London* wrote: 'Chain stores and multiple office buildings and flats have made many parts of London indistinguishable from their equivalents in Birmingham, Coventry and Exeter.'

This statement also applies to Middlesex: the traveller there will have difficulty in distinguishing one High Street from another: Wembley, Wood Green, Hounslow and others all exhibit the same series of multiple stores with identical façades. Office blocks have an equal uniformity of glass, concrete, plastic slabs and aluminium, all

designed to give a maximum occupancy and rent per square foot and varying only in their grandiose entrances. The thousands of factories in the area are more notable for their individualism, but it would be hard to find an architectural masterpiece among them. The post-war schools are more rewarding to the eye: many Middlesex County Schools are well designed, well placed in their surroundings, spacious and full of light. There has been little major municipal building since 1945: in the inter-war years the town halls at Hornsey, Friern Barnet and Wembley stand out as exceptions, among much that is pompous rather than grand. Of smaller municipal buildings, there a few community centres and branch libraries with grace and individuality. The new churches are less interesting than the old: but there are some conspicuous exceptions, especially in Catholic churches. Of all the public buildings, the underground stations still stand out in their simplicity and their supreme fitness of purpose.

The traveller in Middlesex, however, will chiefly have the impression of houses, thousands and thousands of them, sometimes in municipal estates, sometimes built by private enterprise in 'avenues', 'closes', 'rows' or 'ways' (there are few 'streets' or 'roads' in Middlesex). They vary in style: long Victorian terraces; uniform rows of semi-detacheds; bleak municipal estates, their form dictated by economic circumstances; towering blocks of flats. But all this extent of bricks and mortar is mitigated by the hundreds of open spaces and parks, and the generous provision of street trees. Some of the older estates, such as Hampstead Garden Suburb are obvious 'communities' —in others the community spirit scarcely seems to exist.

Raymond Unwin wrote that London is a collection of villages. In spite of the wilderness of bricks and mortar and concrete, the villages of Middlesex still exist, though many have been eroded by time and development. Many of them are hidden, some merely a few cottages round a parish church. The object of the journeys in this book is to find the villages and the churches, the remains of the old manors, and to examine the great houses that still exist. In the search for the villages, I have looked also for traces of the worthies, the men and women (some great, some notorious) who have lived in

3 *Cromwell House, Highgate*

Middlesex, and to show in some measure their relation to history.

So this is a survey made in a series of journeys through the county, mostly along its arterial roads, branching off them to see places of interest. The journeys start on the Essex border with the River Lea, continue on the north where Hertfordshire meets Middlesex. They end in West Middlesex on the Buckinghamshire border, with Surrey and the Thames. The journeys include nine of the new London boroughs: to these are added three urban districts, Potters Bar, Staines and Sunbury, all of them in Middlesex before 1965.

CHAPTER TWO

Along the Lea

The eastern border of Middlesex marches with Essex: it is a natural border, formed by the windings of the River Lea. The division at the south between Tottenham, in Middlesex, and Hackney (in the County of London) is man-made and imperceptible. Stamford Hill and Tottenham High Road form a continuous wide thoroughfare, fringed by flats, houses, shops and small factories. Yet this is the Roman Road, Ermine Street, which ran from Bishopsgate through Tottenham, Edmonton and Waltham Cross to Lincoln. Tottenham High Road looks like many others of its kind: the green verges have largely disappeared, the few seventeenth- or eighteenth-century houses remaining are decaying or have been altered.

But Izaak Walton's Piscator 'stretched his legs up Tottenham Hill' on his long walk to Ware in Hertfordshire, before fishing the higher reaches of the Lea—the 'hill' is the slight rise in the High Road before reaching Tottenham High Cross. The Cross, centre of the old village, was originally of wood. Replaced by brick about 1700, it is now stuccoed and gothicised. The cross figures in a number of eighteenth-century prints, and is still recognisable from them.

Turning up Bruce Grove to the left, where a few of the old Quaker houses retain a battered dignity, one finds in Lordship Lane the best remaining part of the old Tottenham. Bruce Castle stands back from the traffic-laden highway, elegant in its mellow brick. The fine porch and tower surmounted with a cupola, and the two wings, are seventeenth- and eighteenth-century work. The ornate clock, with its primitive mechanism, keeps good time. The north front, looking on the park has a massive pediment containing the arms of Lord Coleraine. A round brick tower of about 1600 was probably part of

5   Henrietta Barnett Memorial and Free Church,
Hampstead Garden Suburb

the original castle: it now houses a prosaic oil tank. Tucked away at the side is a yellow brick Victorian wing built by the Hill family for their school, run on 'modern progressive principles'. The best-known members of the Hill family were Rowland, of the penny post, and Birkbeck Hill, the Johnsonian scholar.

Bruce Castle Park is at its best in the spring: there are some splendid trees, and a sea of varied blossom. The castle itself is now a museum of postal and local history. It houses many relics of the old Post Office, a good collection of coaching prints, and a comprehensive library of books on postal history. The local collection contains the prized Tottenham Court Rolls going back to 1318, together with relics and diaries of various owners, including Lord Coleraine (who grumbled about his decreasing revenues) and Rowland Hill. This in fact, is a compact, unified and unpretentious local museum.

A few yards from the Castle, down Church Lane, is the Priory, a fine seventeenth-century house with eighteenth-century additions. A well-preserved house this: features of the interior are some magnificent decorative plaster ceilings and good panelling, dating from 1620, when the house was built for Joseph Fenton. The Priory is now the vicarage of All Hallow's Church, and may be viewed by appointment. The church, close by, has a fourteenth-century tower and a porch dating from 1500: but there are many later accretions, and considerable restoration of the interior by the Victorian architect William Butterfield. 'Disappointing', writes Pevsner. There are, however, some fine monuments and a splendid French stained-glass window of about 1600.

This small enclave of castle, church and priory is a reminder of Tottenham's history and its connections with Robert Bruce of Scotland, who was lord of the manor. The district had close ties with the Society of Friends. There was a well-known Quaker boarding school here: Priscilla Wakefield's children's savings bank in 1798 was a pioneer effort; while William Hobson, another Quaker resident, was the building contractor for Newgate Prison and the Martello towers. Tottenham has had many historians; among them the remarkable Frederick Fisk, who wrote, printed, bound and sold his history from his own bookshop; there was even a 'farthing history' given out by tradesmen instead of change.

Largely a working-class district built up in the last three decades of the nineteenth century, Tottenham is undistinguished in its architecture (though Pevsner has a kind word to say for the L.C.C. redbrick estate in White Hart Lane). But White Hart Lane is better known as the station for the Tottenham Hotspur football ground. The Borough's 'open spaces' are, for the most part formal and utilitarian, and the random siting of factories has done nothing to improve its amenities.

The prim Victorianism of Northumberland Park, to the right of the High Road should, however, be explored. Here lived Charles Bradlaugh the Victorian freethinker who was expelled, re-elected and excluded from the House of Commons for refusing to take the oath. His name is commemorated on an uncompromising block of flats. Beyond Northumberland Park Station lies Marsh Lane, which leads to the River Lea. Here stood Tottenham's only remaining farmhouse, Asplin's, scheduled as a monument; fallen into decay, its panelling torn out for firewood, it was demolished. Its site is covered by a factory complex and the vast sheds of the Victoria line of London Transport.

Farther down Marsh Lane there is honeysuckle in the hedges and as one reaches Stonebridge Lock, the sleepy atmosphere of the Lea Navigation takes over. Pymmes' Brook, tamed and channelled, flows into the canal. A barge or two and some dinghies are moored on the canal bank.

Crossing the footbridge over the lock, avoiding a sight of the gasworks and the pylons, one might be on the banks of any canal in rural England. The lock-keeper hoes his garden, a lark sings, hedge sparrows abound. May blossom, comfrey, charlock, cow parsley, the common flora of the countryside are all around. This is a land of marsh and reservoirs; millions of gallons of London's water are extracted here; the towers that project from the miniature hills are those of pumping stations. The canal works are of interest—Telford and Smeaton were responsible for some of them. Farther south, at Markfield Road, the industrial archaeologist can find a vintage beam engine of 1886 which the Borough Council has preserved.

The River Lea is no longer navigable, as it was by the Danes in 894—a Danish long boat was found when the nearby Lockwood Reservoir was excavated in 1900. Water extraction has reduced the Lea to a fraction of the river Walton knew; muddy, unclear, with trails of flannel weed, it moves slowly. But there are still shoals of coarse fish, and at week-ends dozens of hopeful anglers and boys line the banks. There are plans for the Lea Valley: a 25-mile stretch of it may become a playground if the Lea Valley Development obtains £30,000,000.

The towpath extends for almost a mile and the rural atmosphere vanishes, with vast works on the left bank. Steel barges, full of huge logs of exotic woods lie on the canal. There are timber yards and busy cranes. There is an overall smell of sawdust, glue and oil; this is one of the centres of the furniture industry. Neat twentieth-century offices alternate with rusty sheds. Vans and lorries move along the towpath. At Angel Road there is a viaduct across the marshes, an enormous block of offices, and the beginning of Edmonton.

Having seen Tottenham in two days' journeying and tramping, waiting on draughty corners, furiously enduring the delays of public transport, I was determined to endure no more. Robbins, I had read, tramped many miles along Middlesex roads, when he wrote his history. I had no desire to emulate him; so I found a willing companion, and my future travels in Middlesex were taken by car. 'The great affair is to move,' wrote R. L. Stevenson—and to see everything in this crowded county one has to move, and fairly fast. To do so with a friend knowledgeable and with a sense of humour, with in addition a genius for parking, made each planned journey a pleasure.

With Edmonton we were to start in Fore Street, the continuation of Tottenham High Road. The approach, by Angel Corner is flanked by two frowning blocks of council flats. But to the left is a haven of quiet from the traffic. Pymme's Park, of 50 or so acres was once graced by an Elizabethan mansion, burnt down in 1940. Only the walled garden now remains, nicely planted with roses and perennials: here the tourist may rest (as my companion and I did) before taking the plunge into Fore Street to see what remains of Antique

Edmonton—the Edmonton of *The Merry Devil, The Witch* and *John Gilpin*. The grave of Peter Fabell—the 'devil' cannot be found in the parish church: while old Elizabeth Sawyer, who was executed for witchcraft in 1621, is recorded, but not commemorated. There is far more trace of John Gilpin to be discovered. Lady Austin told the tale to Cowper, who turned it into galloping verse in 1782. Within three years prints of John Gilpin's Ride were available throughout London, and Edmonton was famous.

Pymme's Brook, which is channelled under Fore Street was 'the wash' which Gilpin

> *... threw about*
> *On both sides of the way*
> *Just like unto a trundling mop*
> *Or a wild goose at play ...*

And the Bell Inn, where John's wife stood shrieking 'Stop! Stop! John Gilpin here's the house' is still on the left of Fore Street, though the scrupulous antiquarian should add that there are eight 'Bell' inns in Edmonton, all competing for this legendary distinction. At any rate, the council flats in Fore Street include a *Gilpin House*.

Fore Street itself is a muddle: three charming little Georgian houses in Angel Place remain, but they are not well cared for. The rest looks like a Victorian working-class district uneasily shrugging itself into the twentieth century. An eighteenth-century chapel is frowned at, across the street, by a hideous congregational church. But the new council flats are nicely designed, with their own neat pub. The 1897 Public Library is dedicated to the memory of Lamb and Keats, with bronze plaques in the hall. Here are housed the collections of the Lamb Society, and a fine selection of local material. I saw there an old photograph of the *Alcazar*, one of the original 'Kinematographs', now replaced by a towering block of flats.

The real literary associations of Edmonton are with John Keats and Charles Lamb. Keats lived with his grandmother in Church Street, and was apprenticed to Hammond, an apothecary and surgeon who practised nearby; his small dwelling was pulled down in 1931, but a plaque (difficult to find) commemorates this in Keats Parade, Church Street. And in this street also is found Lamb's cottage, tucked in by a redbrick nursing home and a carpark, and scarcely visible to the passing motorist. It was here that Elia 'driven from house to house by Mary's illness' came in 1833 to spend his last years. The neat stuccoed cottage is well preserved by its owner, but is not open to the public. There were more difficulties in finding Lamb's tombstone in the overgrown graveyard of All Saint's Parish Church. But, penetrating muddy paths, brushing aside nettles and fireweed, there it was, with Carey's inscription, kept neat and clean:

Farewell dear friend, that smile, that harmless mirth
No more shall gladden our domestic hearth.

All Saint's Church, founded in 1136 by Geoffrey de Mandeville, has undergone much restoration and rebuilding. With havoc from bombs and death-watch beetle, much care and love has gone into the restoration—the fifteenth- and sixteenth-century roofs are to be admired; there are fragments of a Norman doorway, some small brasses, and a few interesting monuments. A number of the bells date back to 1734. The adjacent almshouses have been skilfully rebuilt, and form a pleasant enclave in the churchyard. The Lamb Memorial Hall opposite looked grey and glum in the autumn rain.

A cup of coffee in the Viking restaurant, which surprisingly turned out to have a typically Costa Brava decor, quickly brought me back into this century. Here a builder and his assistant, cheerfully unaware of Lamb and Keats, convinced me that the essence of Edmonton lay in the Old Green, which forms the end of Fore Street. I found a cheerful hugger mugger: shops and market stalls, a railway station, a ring of pubs, and throngs of people; all combined with a frantic traffic jam. Perhaps this was a relic of the Old Edmonton Fair. The few Georgian frontages were scarcely visible behind a line of lorries trying to get into the Hertford Road. Just past the Green is a charming early Victorian crescent with delicate balconies. Most of it was in decay, but number 90 was sleek in fresh paint. The Green and its surround is a Victorian relic, which must be a source of irritation to the planners, but it is a typical London street scene, and an enjoyable one.

Other old houses in Edmonton have to be sought out. Beyond the Cambridge Road in Bury Street lies a seventeenth-century manor in a mass of domestic suburbia: twisted chimneys and pargetted upper storeys, and a medley of vari-shaped windows are the features of this restored Jacobean house set in spacious grounds and now used as an Arts Centre. Evening is the best time for seeing the interior, for many societies meet there. At the top of Bush Hill a mile or so away is Halliwick House, built by Sir Hugh Myddleton, in 1613, towards the end of his work on the New River, which brought Hertfordshire water to London. The centre of the house was part of the original fabric, but there have been many additions. The New River runs at the back of the house, and one finds it again a number of times on the journey through North Middlesex.

The next excursion took me back again to the Lea. This section of Edmonton is a mixture of small houses and industrial estate, though a curious name of an inn. *The Cart Overthrown*, is a reminder that the district was once rural. The Lea is approached through some tipping sites, one of them meant for an 18-hole golf course. Pickett's Lock, near a sewage farm, is on the Lea Navigation. The banks of the canal were peaceful on the hot autumn day when I went there, and a few fishermen lazed in the sun. Harry Mottram the lock-keeper, a compact muscular man, scented officialdom as he saw the map under my arm. Reassured, he relaxed. The lock-keeper's life, he said, was full of incident: only the previous week he had fished his fortieth body from the canal—a suicide. Barge traffic was mainly in the mornings. He pointed out a curiously squat little vessel moored nearby—it was one of the original powder barges. Solidly built of oak, with no metal in its construction, it had been travelling down the Lea from the gunpowder mill for over 200 years. Launched into a discussion of place names, I heard of local lore and legend. On learning what I was doing, Harry confessed to a taste for writing himself—a poem of his had been published in the *Waterman's Journal*. And he recited, with gusto, a poem of his about Canute's preference for wool, which was familiar to me as a Wool Secretariat advertisement. I said goodbye, and was permitted (being semi-official) to drive the car up the tow-path to Ponder's End—a rare privilege.

This is the eastern border of Enfield: a rural spot, if one's back is turned to the vast power station half a mile away. The lock-keeper had told me that this was, literally, Ponder's End—where one Ponder, mistaken for a highwayman, was hanged. The English Place Name Society records it, more soberly, as the end of the parish, where John Ponder lived. Wright's flour mill, rambling and clapboarded, was built in 1713; and there was a mill here in the fourteenth century. There was a steady throb of machinery, a grainy smell, an old mill pond; and though the outhouses which were once stables now contained lorries, it was easy to slip out of the twentieth century. But I soon came back to the present in an endeavour to find Enfield Lock, travelling through a complex of pylons, factories and power stations to Enfield Wash. The Wash itself is tamed, culverted and turgid as it disappears under the high road by Turkey Street. The cottage where Elizabeth Canning was locked up in 1753 by Mother Wells, the alleged procuress, has long ago disappeared. Down Ordnance Road, through a decaying Victorian village is Enfield Lock, close to the northern boundary of Middlesex, where the Lea River and the Lea Navigation separate. The huge reservoirs nearby are difficult to reach except on foot. One authority advocates their use for boating. The county planners talk about a giant incinerator to be built near here.

Down the attractively named Swan and Pike Road I found the Royal Small Arms Factory, home of the Lee-Enfield rifle—the rifle which made the British Empire. The factory was founded by the Board of Ordnance in 1804: but as far back as 1653 gunpowder was made here, as it was at Waltham Abbey a few miles away. The walnut trees that fringe the river are probably the descendants of those planted in 1800 to make gunstocks. The factory is a 'forbidden area' and cannot be visited. But there was little activity that day: the *Royal Ordnance* pub was closed, and Enfield Lock House was shuttered and sleepy.

The centre of Enfield lies well away from the Lea, and is reached through Southbury Road, off the old Hertford Road. Enfield is more like a county town than any other place in North Middlesex. It is now the London Borough of Enfield, amalgamated with Southgate and Edmonton. Along its borders with Essex and Hertfordshire it is still rural, with many small farms and nursery gardens; these, with woods, parks and open spaces were all once part of the vast Enfield Chase. The factories (and there are many of them) are zoned along the Lea and the Cambridge Road. The residential part of Enfield is for the most part sober, respectable, upper-middle class; but there are a number of unexpected charms, some fine houses, many of them hidden from the motorist; and a considerable history. This history goes back to Elizabethan times, and still farther: for 'Enefield' is in Domesday Book and Geoffrey de Mandeville first Earl of Essex, was the first Lord of the Manor.

The Market House with its eight teak pillars commemorates the coronation of Edward VII; but it replaces a much older structure, and there was a market here in the fourteenth century. Beyond the market lie the Grammar School, established in 1557, and St. Andrew's Church. Near here was Enfield Palace, conjecturally of Elizabeth I, demolished in 1928. St. Andrew's has been largely rebuilt, with both inside and outside pleasant and well-cared for. Going inside, the chief feature is a magnificent organ case of 1751. Fine monuments abound—the most remarkable being that of Lady Joyce Tiptoft (1446), with an effigy and a brass. The most conspicuous monument is that of Sir Nicholas Raynton of Forty Hall, and his family, in coloured marble.

Outside, the neatly arranged tombstones on a closely cut lawn, backed by a mellow brick wall, give the impression of care and pride in preserved antiquity which is found in many parts of Enfield. Penetrating a long passage behind the church I came to Gentleman's Row, houses mostly of the early eighteenth century. Through its small gardens meanders the New River. Many of the gardens are separated from the houses by a flagged walk: and I noticed that a number of the porches bore the bronze insignia of the Enfield Preservation Society. Charles Lamb lived in Clarendon Cottage from 1829, then at the cottage next door, before moving to Edmonton in 1833. Brecon House, Elm House, Sedgecope—each has an individual charm;

the elderly lady, Miss Beavan, who lives at Archway cottage claims that her front garden was the original town cockpit. Little Park, a modern villa behind a high wall, contains an Elizabethan Room, where the owner, Major Groves, has preserved the remains of Enfield Palace. There is a remarkable fireplace, handsome panelling, and an ornate plaster ceiling. The room is available for meetings of local societies. There have been rumours from time to time about a ring road that might encroach on the Row. May it long remain as it is— 'highly picturesque and varied', as Pevsner puts it.

Enfield abounds in fine houses, many of them behind high walls: houses which the motorist will never see unless he is willing to slow down and turn into gateways which are, apparently, private. I suppose I must have trespassed occasionally in our journey up Silver Street and Forty Hill: but everyone encountered was courteous. The old vicarage in Silver Street has two wings built in the sixteenth century. Farther on the left is Enfield Court, built about 1690—now the lower school of the grammar school. It was out of term; I found the interior much altered, the panelling much painted: only the ceilings were evidence of some antiquity. The house was part of the original manor of Worcesters. The grounds were spacious: the great cedar of Lebanon (though not the original one planted by Robert Uvedale, the headmaster) was magnificent. The gazebo and circular riding house built by Sir Alfred Somerset have now disappeared.

A slow drive up Forty Hill was a rewarding experience. The splendid wrought-iron gates which once led into Gough Park are well preserved, but lead nowhere. There are half a dozen charming houses including The Hermitage of 1704, Worcester Lodge and the delightful Elsynge Cottage. But Forty Hall is magnificent, not domestic. The council now own it, and are restoring and improving with care, and in good taste. Built by Sir Nicholas Raynton (whose tomb is in the church) its red brick façade dates from about 1630. The swaggering gateway to the stables is attributed to Inigo Jones. The interior has exuberant plaster ceilings, fine panelling and spacious rooms, which house a well-chosen collection of prints, glass and porcelain. The arms of the Bowles family, last lords of the manor, are set in the glass of the staircase window. The parkland grounds are well kept: there is an ornamental lake, and two fine avenues of trees. The site of Elsynge House, where Elizabeth I lived as princess, is nearby, and an elegant little modern art gallery has been arranged in the old stables. This is a house of great character, and a close rival, architecturally, to the more famous Kenwood in Hampstead.

Another Bowles owned Myddleton House, a little farther up the hill—E. A. Bowles, a landscape gardener and horticulturalist; his flagged garden here is famous, full of exotic plants and old fashioned roses. It is a delightful place to visit, with its nooks, archways and unexpected vistas: colchicums bloomed under the trees. The house itself is a medical school. The ubiquitous New River runs close to the grounds, and appears also in Whitewebbs Park, nearby on the left, off Bulls Cross. This is a natural park, with the hand of the municipal gardener scarcely evident. The winding paths go between tall timber, and as I came down to the river, a large white house appeared: French in appearance, it was built in 1791 and subsequently altered. Local tradition associates Whitewebbs with the gunpowder plot of 1605. Modern historians deny it, as they deny the legends about the nearby *King and Tinker* inn, where James I is supposed to have knighted an outspoken tinker.

A single day's visit, however, is not enough to see all the antiquities of Enfield. Enfield Chase is still extensive though most of its fine timber is gone. Once a hunting ground of the Tudor Court, it was siezed in Commonwealth times in order to exploit its timber, but regained in 1660, replanted and stocked with deer. The four lodges which were the entrances to the chase are still there, recognisable, though altered: an interesting afternoon's excursion is to search them out, driving along the Ridgeway. East Lodge, near the curiously named hamlet of Botany Bay, is away from the road, down a muddy path. Once used by Charles I as a hunting lodge, it is now uncared for, and for once my curiosity was not unrewarded. North Lodge, near the water tower is Kilvinton Hall, much altered, but in good trim. The roads around here, especially Cattlegate Lane, are delightful in the early afternoon; but the evening finds them crowded with the cars of commuters, rushing home to Hertfordshire.

West Lodge, where John Evelyn visited Secretary Coventry is spick and span in dazzling paint; the house much expanded is now an excellent hotel. 'It is a very pretty place,' wrote the diarist, 'the house commodious, the gardens handsome. To this lodge there are three great ponds and some few inclosures, the rest a solitary desert, yet stor'd with not less than 3000 deere ... pretty retreats for gentlemen, especially for those who are studious and lovers of privacy.'

Driving along the Ridgeway one is very conscious of the country-side, as Evelyn was—only 14 miles from London. Down Hadley Road I sought out Camlet Moat, an old earthwork mentioned in Scott's *Fortunes of Nigel* as the remnants of a mansion of the Earl of Mande-ville, and rumoured to have been a haunt of Dick Turpin. From the road it was no more than a green tump, fenced in from the curious. To see Trent Park I circuited the chase, arriving at the bustling suburb of Cockfosters. The 'satisfying modern vernacular' of the Underground Station is now dominated by a concrete and glass office building. A long down-hill drive on the left leads to the splendid mansion of Trent Park; originally built by Richard Jebb, doctor to George III, it has been much extended and altered, but always with a sense of style. Sir Edward Sassoon reconstructed and refaced the house with old bricks from William Kent's Devonshire house. Now a busy Teachers' Training College and owned by the Greater London Council, it retains the atmosphere of a great country house, with its park of 1,000 acres, which was originally laid out by Humphry Repton. From Trent Park I sought out South Lodge, now a hospital, and quite unrecognisable as the former residence of William Pitt, Earl of Chatham. The windmill near the house has disappeared. The story has it that the unpainted windmill was offensive to Pitt, who paid for the paint : he paid twice, for the windmill turned, and it was found that the ingenious miller had painted only one half of it.

The chase, associated with hunting, is also famous for horse-breed-ing. The Glasgow Stud Farm on the Ridgeway is the home of the British Bloodstock Agency; the farmhouse itself is of some antiquity, its fine staircase being listed by the Royal Commission for Historical Monuments. I sought long for Major Metcalf's Clydesdale Stud Farm, eventually finding it behind another of Enfield's high walls : but there were no horses, only a few quiet donkeys cropping the grass in the park. The magnificent Victorian stables with wrought-iron gates to the stalls, contained a solitary pony. The house is of the eighteenth century, built for a former Governor of Bombay; the walled garden is now used for horticultural displays by the Enfield College of Technology. Horticulture, in fact, forms still another facet to Enfield's many-sided activities: for Cranfield, Perry and Rochford, known to all gardeners, have their nurseries here.

Enfield with its long history, has many worthies. Sir Walter Raleigh was undoubtedly in attendance on the young princess Elizabeth, though his residence has never been fully established. Keats and Cowden Clarke were at a school near Enfield town station: Isaac D'Israeli, Frederick Marryat, Charles Babbage, Walter Pater—all are associated with the town in Victorian times.

The two villages of Winchmore Hill and Southgate, now incorporated in Enfield, are villages no longer, but retain a few fine houses and two village greens. That of Winchmore Hill, reached from Green Lanes has much charm, with its weatherboarded houses, and small shops—no less than five of them selling antiques. The village has long been associated with the Quakers: George Fox came here often. The present meeting house dates from 1791, and in its burial ground are to be found many Freames and Goulds, the founders of Barclay's Bank, and the ancestors of another great banking family, the Hoares. The district is pleasant and hilly, and though Winchmore Hill Wood has long disappeared, an unusual number of forest trees line the avenues, which have curious names such as Green Dragon Lane, Park Ridings, Worlds End Lane, and so on. It was down the Bourne that I found Grovelands Park, formerly the old deer park, subsequently landscaped by Humphry Repton. The house nearby is a magnificent John Nash villa with four great Ionic columns which look out on the park. The house is now a hospital. Not far from here is Southgate, with its circular underground station and crescent of shops: the High Street is developed with its rather stark technical college, but the Green nearby has much charm. The Georgian Minchenden House School was once the residence of Sir John Lawrence, Governor-General of India. The *Cherry Tree Inn*—a local landmark—was first licenced in the reign of George II. Past the Green and on Alderman's Hill is Broomfield Park.

Broomfield House, of the seventeenth century, sits in a fine park with some noble trees. The exterior of the house is conglomerate, with much restoration. Inside, it is a local museum, devoted entirely to Southgate material, and quite evidently well looked after by its voluntary curators. The chief architectural feature is a fine timbered staircase, embellished by allegorical frescoes by Lanscroon (some say by Sir James Thornhill): whoever painted them, they give an air of grandeur to this neat and attractive mansion, where the old kitchen houses a small art gallery. There are many local prints and water-colours on display; and finding that a number of them concerned the famous Walkers, a cricketing family, I set out to find the Walker family residence. Arnos Grove, now renamed Northmet House, is on Cannon Hill: and to outward view is simply a neo-Georgian block of offices. But the central portion is the house, built in 1719, where a tablet commemorates the Walkers, who lived here for 130 years. Within, the spacious hall was silent: a kind receptionist allowed me to see the murals (really by Lanscroon this time—they are fine): 'Dark and baroque', writes Pevsner. I was even allowed to see the fine Adam board room, with its half circle of columns. The Victorian Walkers were the cricketers: and in a series of great three-day matches from 1858-63, the Southgate cricket team were able to take on all-England elevens. John, Alfred, Frederick, Arthur, Henry, Vyell Edward, Russell Donisthorne, Isaac Donisthorne—all played for Southgate. Only Vyell Edward (1837-1906) appears in the *Dictionary of National Biography*—he was according to Lillywhite 'the best all-round cricketer in the world'.

Southgate and Winchmore Hill, then, will bring a few rewards to the explorer: 'a prime specimen of Middlesex', wrote Leigh Hunt, who was born there.

CHAPTER THREE

Northern Heights—
and onwards

Seven Sisters Road and Green Lanes sound countrified enough, but the lanes are no longer green, all built up as far as Southgate; and the seven trees which gave the road its name disappeared long ago. This part of the new London Borough of Haringey, known as Finsbury Park, doesn't know whether to decay or not; the tube and railway station seem to have cast a blight around it. The old Empire, once a flourishing palace of varieties is shut and barred, while a vast cinema, the Astoria only occasionally is crowded. On the other hand, there is a good modern hotel—a rarity in this part of Greater London.

Finsbury Park itself, 120 acres of green and trees is an oasis in a two-mile length of urban sprawl and undistinguished building. In the Park are the penultimate windings of the New River met in Enfield. The boating lake is extensive; it was once called Hornsey Wood Lake, and near it was Hornsey Wood Tavern, resort of the cockney sportsmen portrayed by Gillray in a series of caricatures. This was a celebrated tavern, its ordinaries famous—'hot roast and boiled every day from two to five'—and its name crops up in some of the sporting literature of early Victorian times. All this vanished when the tavern was demolished. What remains is a well kept and reasonably sedate public park.

Passing the park and moving up Green Lanes on the right, is the vast hulk of Harringay Stadium, with its greyhound racing track. The stadium has housed all sorts of gatherings—even Eugene Ormandy and the Philadelphia Orchestra—but the name Haringey (its proper spelling) inevitably suggests 'the dogs'. So much so, that

when the new London Borough was formed, a greyhound was embodied in the proposed civic arms. Indignant councillors would have
nothing of it—and the insignia now embody a spark, denoting tele-
vision. The left side of Green Lanes contains no less than 27 roads,
parallel and interlacing, all of them very similar in style, marching
up to the miniature height of Stroud Green. All were built between
1886 and 1900; all are in variegated brick with artificial stone facings.
But even here there must have been someone with a romantic turn
of mind, for a small enclave near the park contains six roads named
after Disraeli's heroes and heroines: Alroy, Endymion, Coningsby,
Lothair, Tancred and Venetia. This part of the old Borough of Hornsey is cut off from the rest by the old North Eastern Railway line and
a huge marshalling yard, while the open channel of the New River
runs behind the roads, unexpectedly appearing here and there.

Coming up to Turnpike Lane, there is one welcome piece of the
twentieth century in this rather tired wilderness. A little off to the
right is Milton Road, a tiny modern community housing 390 people
—not in the usual glaring block of flats, but in neat little houses and
two-storey apartments, compact, charming and secluded. In the
paved precinct young trees have been planted. Here is an example
of what real architectural imagination can do—for spaciousness has
been achieved, although there are 100 people to the acre.

The next patch of green is Duckett's Common, named after an
ancient manor; a green thronged with pigeons and toddlers. This is
Turnpike Lane. One of Charles Holden's finer tube stations, it is no
longer the 'pretty group' admired by Pevsner, being obscured by alterations, road furniture, and too much traffic.

Here Green Lanes becomes High Road Wood Green, the largest
shopping centre in North London—perhaps there is nothing more to
be said, for shopping centres, large or small, are very much alike.
This one does, however, contain one of London's most remarkable
bespoke tailors who, starting here from nothing, has now graduated
to Savile Row. Wood Green, detached from Tottenham in 1888, became a borough in 1933, and reunited with Tottenham and Hornsey
in 1965 to become the London Borough of Haringey.

'There is indeed nothing in the Borough worth more than a cursory

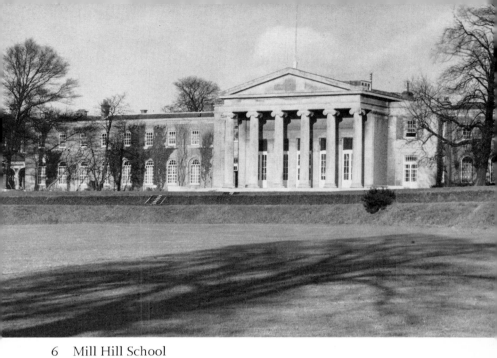

6   Mill Hill School

7   Harrow School

glance,' says our most eminent authority. One or two churches and the almshouses may be of interest to the amateur of Victorian architecture; all of the old hamlet has disappeared; and the *Three Jolly Butchers* (of 1798) is now chromiumed up to the eaves. There is indeed a scheme to transform the area round the station, the public library, and the little open space known as Spouter's Corner into a large municipal and shopping precinct. If it shows the same imagination as Milton Road it will be worth seeing.

But Wood Green does contain one curiosity in the shape of Alexandra Park and Palace. The Alexandra Palace, the white mastodon of North London, was in trouble from its beginnings. Within 14 days of its opening in May 1873, there was a devastating fire. With true Victorian energy it was rebuilt and reopened in May 1875. This huge building, in a park of over 170 acres seems to have had shaky finances from the beginning, and was purchased by the Middlesex County Council and five neighbouring authorities in 1900. The dream of a huge community centre for North London never became a reality, and its vast halls were never completely occupied at one time. Prisoners of war were interned there in World War I, refugees received there in 1940. The B.B.C. leased some of the Palace in 1935 and used it to inaugurate the television service; today the B.B.C. wing is the only part of the palace in which there is continuous activity. The Great Hall is seldom occupied, and the immense organ (long disused) may be sold. So this huge greying hulk, half Italianate stone, half glass, lies on the heights, melancholy, deserted and decaying.

The park is well kept by the Greater London Council, its new owners, and the terrace, 300 feet up, gives a fine view of London, and, in the valley, of the whole of the old Borough of Hornsey, from the former Hornsey Village to the heights of Highgate. The view is chiefly of grey roofs with terraced houses marching up and down hills, but conspicuous also are some open spaces, and thousands of street trees. Deep down on the left is the tower of Hornsey Church, so I went down the hill to see what was left of Hornsey Village. Of the little that is left, Eagle Court is decently kept, but is now offices. The Victorian rectory has gone, replaced by a glass and concrete school; the *Three Compasses*, famous as a coaching inn, is completely

8   *Chandos Mausoleum, St. Laurence Church, Whitchurch*

rebuilt. Even St. Mary's Church was being demolished to make way for a new church, the fifth on the site. The church tower of 1500 remains, well preserved—the white stones inserted in the brick came from the Bishop of London's hunting lodge in Highgate: in the fifteenth century all of Hornsey was his manor, and Hornsey Great Park his hunting ground. There seems to be just a trace of village left here: the shops are small and unpretentious; there is a horse trough and a clump of trees in the middle of the High Street; and the New River flows placidly by the railway bridge near Hornsey Station. Arnold Bennett, who lodged in Ribblesdale Road during his early years in London, wrote an excellent description of Hornsey Station in *Hilda Lessways*.

Going down Tottenham Lane to Crouch End, I was soon in the familiar world of multiple shops and supermarkets: but the neat civic precinct beyond the Clock Tower is worth more than a glance. Uren's Hornsey Town Hall, built in 1935, is imposing without being overpowering; free from ornament it gets its effects from good massing and superb brickwork. The central library nearby is a worthy companion. Two steep hills run down to Crouch End. At the top of the tree-lined Crouch End Hill stands a rather nondescript collection of buildings, the Hornsey College of Art. This sober-looking place was the scene of many student rebellions, lockouts and stay-ins, one of which lasted 27 days. Normally full of activity, the college is famous for its unusual and advanced courses in applied arts; the students in motley costume, lugging large portfolios, are a familiar sight in this neighbourhood.

Out of Crouch End and into Park Road I made for yet another hill, Muswell Hill, lined with great trees and one of the steepest in London. At its foot lived Thomas Moore while writing *Lalla Rookh*, after which he named his cottage. At Grove Lodge on the right, half way up the hill, lived William Henry Ashurst. Here he gave hospitality to Mazzini, and propagandised for the penny post. At the top of the hill lies a small park called the Grove.

In the forward part, near the *Green Man*, stood Bath House, its owner the notorious Laurence Shirley, fourth Earl Ferrers, who murdered his steward and was hanged at Tyburn in 1760, after a trial by his peers. A later mansion in the grove was occupied by Topham Beauclerk, who lived here in great style, with an astronomer resident, and a vast library that 'stretched from Bloomsbury to Highgate'. Johnson and Boswell visited him here, and I have met an old Muswell Hill inhabitant who pointed out 'Johnson's Walk'.

But the oldest story in Muswell Hill is of the holy well, a place of pilgrimage in medieval times, in the care of the nuns of Clerkenwell. The water had curative properties, and legend has it that King Malcolm IV of Scotland visited the well. There is nothing to be seen, of course, at the house in Muswell Road where the well once stood, for long ago it was bricked up—but perforce I had to look at it. A large portion of this part of Muswell Hill belonged to the Borough of Clerkenwell until 1900, and was known as 'Clerkenwell detached'. And it was curious to reflect that this 'mossy well' had given its name to the whole district.

The late-Victorian shopping centre at Muswell Hill has one merit: it is all of a piece and has a beginning and an ending—'a period piece of unruffled cheerfulness,' says Ian Nairn. The views down the side streets, though urban, are fascinating. In Victorian times many 'worthies', Mudie the librarian, Tegetmeier the naturalist, W. E. Henley, Coventry Patmore, Frederick Harrison, all lived here. Now the district is a brisk and busy middle-class suburb. Throughout the spring and summer the 'street gardens' are conspicuous, with their massed beds of flowers. There are 120 of them, provided by an imaginative council. Through this brisk Broadway then, and down Muswell Hill Road I went, past the fine spire of St. James Church, and towards Highgate. The two avenues on the left Woodland Rise and Woodland Gardens, mark the site of Frederick Lehmann's 'country home', where he entertained many literary men and women in Victorian times. Wilkie Collins stayed here while writing *Man and Wife*, and the mansion was the scene of many brilliant parties. I had to be content with a photograph shown to me by one of the older residents, and a glimpse of the vinery, still there and visible from the road. Just past here, the road runs through woods, with Highgate Wood on the right, Queen's Wood on the left. Here is Archway Road, thunderous with traffic, mainly lorries going north. The *Wood-*

man, once a staging house for coaches, bears no resemblance to the picturesque inn on the Pollard print *A View on the Highgate Road*.

Going up the steep Southwood Lane, we approach Highgate Village. General Wade lived in Southwood Lane, as did Henry Kingsley and his sister Mary (commemorated in Kingsley Place). There is a charming row of almshouses of 1723, and at the end of the lane, with the brick buildings of Highgate School, we are in Highgate Village, the most historic and the best preserved section of the Northern Heights.

Highgate Village is partly in Middlesex, partly in the greater London borough of Camden, but it is quite evident that the residents act as a community, disregarding borough boundaries. There is a strong preservation society, which took effective action when it was proposed to turn the High Street into a 'lorry route'. The village still resembles a village, except in morning and evening rush hours, when it is choked with cars: so visit in the morning or afternoon. Pond Square, full of well preserved Georgian buildings, has great charm. The Grove, mostly eighteenth century, has had many notable residents. At number 3, Samuel Taylor Coleridge lived from 1816 until his death in 1834. St. Michael's Church of 1832, replaced the old Highgate Chapel: one of its most notable features is a splendid modern stained-glass window by Evie Hone. The view down the steep West Hill, looking over Hampstead Heath, is green and pleasant. Beyond the curve is Millfield Lane, where Coleridge and Keats met for the first time. Highgate in Edwardian times, seen through the eyes of a small boy, is beautifully evoked by John Betjeman in *Summoned by Bells*. But this part of Highgate is over the Middlesex border.

The High Street and Hill are the backbone of the village, with half way down a splendid view of London. The roll of Highgate's former aristocratic residents, set forth by Howitt, one of the local historians, reads like an excerpt from Debrett: 'Dorchester, Arundel, Cholmeley, St. Albans, Landerdale, Argyll, Bute, Mansfield, Russell, Southampton.' Few of them have left much trace except in street names. Cromwell and Ireton House, two notable Jacobean houses farther down the hill, were only indirectly connected with the Protector, in spite of their names. Cromwell House, built for Richard Sprignell, a city merchant, has a fine interior with ornate plaster ceilings and a splendid carved oak staircase. The two houses, with many others around are scheduled as historic monuments. Opposite was the home of Nell Gwynn—for she lived in Lauderdale House, the tea-house of Waterlow Park, now rebuilt after a fire. On the long brick wall forming the boundary of the park is a plaque commemorating Andrew Marvell. Here was his cottage, and the garden

> *So with roses overgrown*
> *And, lillies, that you would it guess*
> *To be a little wilderness*

Before going back to the village, one has to visit the Archway down Hornsey Lane, to see the most spectacular view of London. Hans Christian Andersen on his first visit to England, was astonished, when he drove over by night to see 'the great world metropolis mapped out in fire below him'. This was from the old stone arch which was designed by John Nash and replaced in 1897 by the present steel structure. The view, 60 feet above the roaring traffic on Telford's Archway Road, extends down river to Dagenham and the Essex marches with St. Paul's, the City and its new skyscrapers in the middle distance, and at night it is just as fine as the one seen by Andersen.

North Road, near the top of the hill, is a curious mixture of antique and modern, with the red Victorian brick of Highgate School on its right-hand side. In a graveyard here, Coleridge was buried in 1834, the tomb being later transferred to the crypt of the school chapel in 1866. The tomb was neglected for many years until its scandalous disrepair was publicised by the novelist Ernest Raymond. An impressive ceremony was held in 1961 when the coffin was re-interred in St. Michael's, and John Masefield delivered a fine oration; the tomb in the centre aisle of the church has a fine incised inscription by Reynolds Stone. Highgate School was founded as a 'free grammar school' by Sir Roger Cholmeley in 1565. Today its houses and playing fields occupy a long stretch of the nearby Hampstead Lane. One of its more unusual scholars was Gerald Manley Hopkins, who was there from 1854 to 1863, winning the poetry prize in 1860. And it is pleasant to reflect on two more poets who were here—for one day in 1916 the English master, T. S. Eliot, was handed by one of his pupils a tiny notebook—*The Best of Betjeman*.

Highgate has always been a resort of literary men, however: and it was in Byron Cottage in North Hill in 1894 that A. E. Housman lived while writing *A Shropshire Lad*. He did much walking on the Heath and Highgate Woods, and was affronted when the brushwood was cleared from the centre of the wood, giving too much of a view of Archway Road. 'Now when we stand in the centre,' he wrote to the *Standard*, 'we can divide our attention between Juggins' porter and our neighbours' washing. Scarlet flannel petticoats are much worn in Archway Road, and if anyone desires to feast his eyes on these picturesque objects ... let him repair to the centre of High-gate Wood!' So Housman also was one of the Highgate preserva-tionists.

Farther down is the *Bull*, where George Morland stayed, drinking much gin and selling paintings to support himself. There is reputed to be a Morland painting somewhere on the premises, but I have never met anyone who has seen it. There is preserved here, however, an old signature book in which Byron, Dickens and others inscribed their names after assisting at the rather curious ceremony of 'swearing on the horns'—a custom prevalent here and at other Highgate Inns. North Hill is also notable for one monument of twentieth-century architecture: Tecton and Lubetkin's Highpoint, two cream cliffs of concrete flats, splendidly arrogant in their modernity, though they were built in 1936 and 1938. Opposite a larger, but much more timid block of council flats sits uneasily. So down the hill, with a good many pleasant (and expensively restored) houses to admire. We are back to the hubbub of traffic and Aylmer Road, yet another spur to the ubiquitous North Circular. To the left we glimpse the green of Highgate Golf Club. Here, almost where the club-house stands was the site of the Bishop of London's hunting lodge, whose stones are seen in Hornsey's church tower.

Aylmer Road leads into Bishop's Avenue, named after the hunting lodge. The Avenue is of large and opulent houses with extensive grounds, each one vying with the other in the magnificence of garden or elegance of decor. Some are a blazing white, one a delicate shade of pink, yet another floodlit by night; while all sorts of celebrities or notorieties, from Gracie Fields to Savundra have lived here. The parallel Winnington Road is equally opulent.

The chief virtue of Bishop's Avenue is that it leads to Kenwood House. Outside Middlesex as it is, the house must not be missed by anyone visiting Highgate. Enlarged for the Earl of Mansfield by Robert Adam in 1767, the house is splendid, but never overpowering. The red and gold library, with its painted ceiling by Zucchi, is surely one of Adam's finest rooms. The Iveagh collection of paintings is excellently housed here and there are always knots of admirers round the Rembrandt self portrait, the Vermeer *Guitar player* or Gainsborough's *Countess Howe*. The house is finely set in grounds with lawns, great trees and a lake, and there is nothing more pleasant than to sit on the terrace on a sunny afternoon on one of the great teak benches, all presented by admirers of Kenwood. The mansion was Lord Mansfield's country house: in 1780 during the Gordon Riots, the mob having burnt his town house, proceeded towards Highgate to do further destruction. But the ingenious landlord of *The Spaniards Inn* offered them free ale: further supplies were hurriedly rolled up from the Kenwood cellars; and by the time the mob had had their fill, a detachment of Life Guards had come on the scene. And here, only a few hundred yards away from Kenwood is the weatherboarded *Spaniards* on the Finchley and Middlesex border. 'More like a German beer garden than anywhere else I know in London,' declares the appreciative Ian Nairn: long may it stand there; and so may the curious toll house opposite. There has been much controversy about this curious little building: the 'improvers' would have it removed so that traffic could speed through to Hampstead Lane; the preservationists are, so far, winning.

Here we are on the borders of Finchley, and in the London Borough of Barnet. So to see something of Finchley, I went down Bishop's Avenue again, and into Aylmer Road and Falloden Way: these two roads, which are lined with expensive-looking detached

47

houses and blocks of flats, are now becoming another traffic lane between the North Circular and Great North Roads. Wide as they are, they are to become even wider, with six lanes of traffic. At present, there is much green and many trees, and the Mutton Brook that formed the border has been cleverly used in a series of sunken gardens with willows aslant the brook. How long these amenities will remain is doubtful : the motorist has no time to admire them. Here on the left is one of Finchley's landmarks, a remarkable statue, 'La Délivrance', sculpted by Guillaume, 15 feet high, and flourishing a sword. She celebrates the Battle of the Marne, and was presented to the Borough by Viscount Rothermere. Known throughout this part of North London as the Naked Lady, she is a favourite meeting place. Nearby, I revisited another of Finchley's curiosities : College Farm and its model herd of cows, maintained by the Express Dairy Company. Periodically, one may see the cows being milked. There is a neat little huddle of farm buildings; calves peer from the stalls; a notice reads 'Beware of the bull'. Near the spruce little dairy museum one may even buy a glass of milk—and everything smells deliciously of the farm : all this, with the North Circular Road a hundred yards away. But this charming place may soon disappear.

Up Regent's Park Road and Ballards Lane lies the oldest part of Finchley, Church End. There is not a great deal of it, but it is comparatively quiet after the bustle of the High Road nearby. Park House, neat, well preserved, faces vast and gloomy Christ's College. The Church of St. Mary, war-damaged and partly rebuilt, has a fifteenth-century tower, recognisable from old engravings. Inside there is a fine nave, with a splendid fifteenth-century roof. There are some good and well-preserved brasses, some fine memorials, conspicuous among them one to Alexander Kinge (1616). Equally interesting is the delightful twentieth-century branch library next door, where low windows reveal an inviting array of books, luring the reader in. Libraries should always issue this invitation—but not many do; this one, Hornsey, and two at Enfield were exceptions. Down Hendon Avenue to Dollis Brook (another boundary) lies a miniature village. Two greens, a few fine trees and some 50 neat houses are grouped around : whitewash, pebble-dash, an overall atmosphere of peace and domesticity. The architect, one Stratton, is uncelebrated, but someone thought well of him, for there is a pillar bearing his name.

Finchley started to develop in the eighteen-eighties; by then most of the notorious Finchley Common had been built over. It once stretched from East Finchley to Muswell Hill and Friern Barnet. Now a tract of rough untended tract, gorse, bracken, stunted trees of haw-thorn and hornbeam—49 acres of open space, known to Finchleians as the Glebe Land, are the remnants of the Common, preserved by the act of some imaginative council. On the common General Monk drew up his forces in 1660. Somewhere between here and East Finchley troops and volunteers assembled in 1745, for Prince Charles Edward was at Derby and London in a panic—Hogarth satirised this later assembly in his *March to Finchley*. And at all times this was the resort of highwaymen; Duval and Turpin roamed here, and Jack Sheppard was captured in 1724. 'I shall not trust my throat in Finchley Common in the dark,' wrote Lord Minto to his wife. All this was difficult to imagine on a sunny afternoon on the edge of the North Circular Road: but even this remnant of the common must be an eerie place after dark. The *Old White Lion* looks, alas, like any roadhouse, and nothing like the inn portrayed by Pollard. The great oak named after Turpin has disappeared.

The East End Road winds pleasantly into the remnant of a little village, with a tiny green and a nice inn: the *Five Bells*, dating from 1812. Park Farm House and its eighteenth-century barn have gone. Opposite the Finchley cricket ground a high and obviously old wall concealed a convent: a gracious and symmetrical building in rose-red brick, with a good portico. The only trace of its antiquity is on two rainwater heads, dated 1723. This was the old Finchley Manor House—well worth a detour. Farther down is found a pompous Victorian building—Avenue House—bequeathed to Finchley by H. C. Stephens, the ink manufacturers. There are many styles in the building, but a substratum is Italian. Its ten acre park is quite a little gem, with winding paths, rolling lawns, and exotic trees.

Once through the shopping centre at Muswell Hill, the road widens, with Victorian villas on one side, and runs down the hill towards Friern Barnet. A handsome modern pub on the right is named *The Minstrel Boy*, after Thomas Moore. Crossing the inevitable arterial road (yet another flyover is threatened here) we come to the four acre grounds of the old 'Colney Hatch' now renamed Friern Hospital. Opened in 1851, its buildings, its wards and its modern methods were described rather unctuously by Walford in *Greater London*: but the cockneys soon started using the name as a simile for lunacy. It has no validity today. Farther on is the pleasant-looking Friern Barnet Town Hall, now only one of a series of municipal offices of the London Borough of Barnet.

'Friern Barnet has no history,' writes one authority. True, there is little sign of history in Friern Barnet Lane, the 'show road' where handsome houses are set well back against wide grass verges. But the doorway of the church of St. James the Great is twelfth century, the Friary Park was once the site of a Priory belonging to the Hospitallers of St. John, and the great trees are a reminder that this district was once part of the great Middlesex forest, in which Elizabeth I once hunted. A pillar beside the road records the site of a well from which Elizabeth drank, and there is a row of almshouses, much restored, which date from 1612.

Turning the corner, is the Great North Road, at Whetstone, looking like any other shopping centre. The name Whetstone is literal, for tradition has it that there was a great stone here, on which the soldiery whetted their swords prior to the Battle of Barnet in 1471. The inns multiply—*Griffin, Hand and Tower, Black Bull, Black Swan, Bull and Butcher*—all of them old coaching inns, we are told, but only the *Griffin* showing signs of antiquity. It is a curious facet of local history that among the few permanent fixtures in an ever changing topography are the pubs—and Whetstone is no exception. And here we come across a modern phenomenon—tower blocks of offices. The two in Whetstone, Northway House and Ever Ready House, are lumpy and graceless: but all of these office blocks are the result of a deliberate planning decision by the Middlesex County Council. Placed near transport centres, with access to 'pockets' of white collar workers, they have been a success as far as decentralisation is concerned. There are six of them in this part of North Middlesex.

So out of Whetstone and the old Middlesex, and into Barnet, continuing along the Great North Road. Oliver Twist sat on a doorstep here 'wondering at the great number of public houses'. I did, too, for there were seven in less than a mile of road. Barnet now pullulates with shops, supermarkets and shoppers; the battlemented church frowns at the steel and glass of Barnet College. Barnet Vale is largely built over.

It was not until Hadley Green that the countryside felt near. A pub briskly advertised 'Hot vittles' and a notice read 'No horse riding on this land'. Hadley Green has great charm: the tourist should pause to look at a neat semicircle of early Victorian houses, in one of which lived David Livingstone. There is little of Hadley Wood left, and the charm of nightingales that sang there (15 years ago). 'Here was fought the famous battle of Barnet' reads the inscription on an obelisk on a green at the junction of Kitts End Road. Here in 1471 Warwick of Lancaster and his army made their last stand against the men of Edward of York: and Warwick died, according to most accounts, some 20 yards from the obelisk. The monument was erected here by a Sir S. Sambrooke who lived a few miles away at North Mymms. And the hedge on the golf course marks the place where Warwick's army formed up.

The 'bar' at Potter's Bar, the northernmost place in old Middlesex, was yet another entrance to Enfield Chase. The road names are countrified: Wagon Road, Dove lane, Mutton Lane, Kitts End, Dancer's Hill. The gates of Wrotham Park are near the little settlement of Bentley Heath. The house (which cannot be viewed without permission) is of grey stucco, symmetrical, with Ionic columns, arms and decorations on the pediment above—all very impressive. It was built in 1754 for the ill-fated Admiral Byng. The front elevation, which is reached through a garden gate, is the most impressive. Real grandeur was here, with four more tall Ionic columns, a still larger entablature with Neptune, dolphins and other emblems of the sea, and two fine staircases flanking the central feature. The view from the portico is of lawns, rolling fields, fine trees, and in the far distance one house, exactly in the right place. Fine landscaping this: and the pylons which stride round the countryside here are nowhere visible.

To find Dyrham is more difficult, for the grandiose entrance gates in Trotter's Bottom, are tightly shut and seem to lead nowhere. The real entrance has a notice that guard dogs are on patrol; but along the drive a fine nineteenth-century house with a pillared portico is disclosed. Formerly the seat of the Dyrham family, this is a country club and golf course. The two estates of Wrotham and Dyrham with the adjoining lands total over 1,400 acres, and well preserved as they are, ensure the rurality of quite a considerable portion of Potter's Bar. Quite close to here, off the St. Albans Road is Knightsland, a sixteenth-century farm, and the original home of Admiral Byng. This is only glimpsed from the road. The interior contains some fine panelling. And there is a remarkable feature, a series of wall-paintings representing the parable of the Prodigal Son—a feature nobody seems to have satisfactorily explained.

The way to South Mimms (or Mymms) was beset by difficulties. The Barnet by-pass, the St. Albans Road and a spur to the motorway led by a roundabout route to the little village, the northernmost in Middlesex. I remembered it, some 20 years ago as a good place to end a country walk. Today, hemmed in by arterial roads, it seems isolated. The name, say the authorities, 'must remain a mystery'; but its history goes back to the twelfth century. Both the eighteenth-century inns were quite unrecognisable as such from the outside, though there is some fine work inside. The list of vicars inside the church goes back to 1365: prior to that it was served by the Abbey of Walden. There is a thirteenth-century chancel, and some fine brasses and memorials to the Frowyck family, the earliest of them dated 1386. The massive church chest is the earliest piece of furniture in Middlesex, and some lovely Tudor glass glows in a wall. By the porch is a massive tomb, glaring with skulls and other intimations of mortality. The neat, tidy but unremarkable village includes a 'Frowyck Crescent'. Other antiquities near here are Mimms Hall and Blanche Farm, both mentioned by the Royal Commission on Historical Monuments.

It is comparatively easy to find Baker's Lane and Sawyer's Lane, though I failed to see the Roman Road near here, where Hertfordshire and Middlesex join. Baker's Lane is built up, as is Mutton Lane, with factories and a large block of offices. In the centre of Potter's Bar the cross roads are thronged with traffic, the High Street busy: here in the last 30 or so years, another village has disappeared. The only trace of it left is the Manor House, well concealed behind a car-park. Wyllyott's manor has black oak timbers, with much of the Tudor brick remaining: some of the restoration has been far from skilful, with badly matching Flettons instead of the mellow red brick. But it is a picturesque creeper-covered place, well-kept, for it houses an Engineers and Surveyor's department. The chief event in Potter's Bar history was not in the sixteenth, but the twentieth century. It was the Zeppelin: one of two shot down in 1916, the other being at the nearby village of Cuffley. There are many North London people now in their sixties, who will tell you of being awakened from their sleep, as children, to see the monster come flaming from the sky. The crew of both the airships are buried in the churchyard of Potter's Bar, and 35 tablets on the church wall record their names.

CHAPTER FOUR

Hendon and Mill Hill

Hendon is a large borough, seven miles long, three miles wide: the new Borough of Barnet in which it is incorporated extends to 22,000 acres, with a population of over 300,000. It is a district almost entirely of the twentieth century, in Victorian times merely a series of scattered villages. In its southern part it merges into the metropolitan area, while the north opens up into London's Green Belt in the green spaces of Mill Hill and parts of Edgware. In spite of its modernity it has links with medieval history: 'Handone', at the high down, is in Domesday Book.

But before making for the villages and the open spaces, we may look at a modern village, the Hampstead Garden Suburb, which is reached via the North Circular Road and the Finchley Road. The suburb is a thing in itself, now built up and no longer developing. Letchworth and Bedford Park were its predecessors, but Hampstead Garden Suburb is the true fulfilment of Ebenezer Howard's idea of a garden city. And its accomplishment was brought about by the foresight, singlemindedness and pertinacity, amounting to genius, of Henrietta Barnett. She and her husband lived in a cottage on Hampstead Heath, and hearing well in advance of the possible extension of the Hampstead tube, she determined to buy up land, preserving as much open space as possible. She wished to build a 'planned community' for all classes. Raymond Unwin, planner of Letchworth, was the man she chose to carry out her ideas—and he and Barry Parker, with Edwin Lutyens as consultant, accomplished them.

The suburb is a pleasant place—the houses are varied and colourful in their mellow brick, there are no fences, only dwarf walls and hedges. The plan of the streets is varied: there are many crescents and closes, following the contours of the land, with detached, semi-detached and terrace houses intermingled. Buildings 'turn corners as though they were meant to', as Robbins wrote. There is little noise, little through traffic, green lawns, and old trees everywhere. The Central Square has Lutyens' St. Jude's Church, the fine spire of which can be seen for miles around; it has a Free Church, the Institute, the Henrietta Barnett School and other public buildings. There is a sense of dignity and space. Outside the Institute, appropriately, is the memorial to Henrietta Barnett. The Suburb is a place to walk around: roads can be crossed slowly, and many of the avenues are linked by pedestrian walks. Two woods—Little Wood and Big Wood —have been incorporated into the plan and birds abound in the gardens near them. Admittedly the shops are too far away; admittedly many of the roads have become car-parks; but such peace and quiet half a mile from the teeming Finchley Road is something to be jealously preserved, as the residents are undoubtedly aware. And this is still a mixed community—every type from Baronets and future cabinet ministers to aged ladies and retired clerks lived and are living here. It is said that the paternalism of the former estate agents has changed somewhat with changes of ownership of the Suburb, but there still exists a strong sense of community and citizen friendship. There was a Jubilee Festival here in 1957, with exhibitions, plays, the visit of a princess and many other festivities in which people associated with the suburb took part. 'The most nearly perfect example of that English invention and speciality the garden suburb,' writes Pevsner.

Golders Green is brisk, bustling: urban, rather than suburban. Up North End Road, towards the Hampstead Heath extension, there is indeed the remnant of a former village. The celebrated *Bull and Bush* Inn is here, very crowded on Bank Holidays. There is a 'ghost' tube station, never opened, underneath the inn, and the rumble of tube trains may be heard in the bar. This is in fact the village of Golders Hill; the origin of the name coming from a family probably

called Godere; and the place celebrated by Mark Akenside in one of
his odes:

> *Now call the sprightly breezes round*
> *Dissolve this rigid cough profound*
> *And bid the springs of life with gentler movement play*

And in Golders Hill Park are the 'verdant scenes' he admired when
he lived here, with 'Mungo' Dyson in the mansion, Golders Hill
House. The park is a gem, with a profusion of fine trees, including
Ginkos and Tulips; the grounds were laid out by Capability Brown;
and there is a small herd of deer. Some tenants of the houses nearby
used to have private keys to the park. Not far away is Ivy House,
where Anna Pavlova lived for many years. The Waugh family lived
at 145 North End Road, and there are glimpses of the life here in the
early years of this century in Alec Waugh's autobiography. Golders
Hill is less than peaceful today, and North End Road is full of
traffic: going down the hill, and towards the Clock Tower, one has
to move fast.

Golders Green Road, a busy shopping centre, is architecturally
null, but beneath its commercialism there is something exotic. On
Saturday mornings the pavements are crowded with superbly clad
Jewish families coming away from *Shool*, who parade, or stand chat-
ting in groups. (Hendon contains 15 synagogues.) The food shops and
delicatessen are superb, with exotic salamis, Prague ham and caviare
as readily available as the more homely *matzos* and *Bagels*. There
is a rainbow of shoeshops, with the names of Ferragamo, Bally and
Gucci prominent; while the jewellers are of Bond Street standard.
Evelyn Waugh hated this district, and had his letters posted in
Hampstead—I thought it was fun. A steep hill ends Golders Green
Road. Turning to the right with the culverted Dollis Brook bordering the road we come to Great North Way and to Hendon Hall.

Here was the country residence of David Garrick, who was lord of
the Manor of Hendon in 1756, and who lived here until 1778,
apparently in great style. Although Garrick later rued his purchase, it
gave him status: with it went the vicarial patronage of St. Mary's

9   Boston Manor, Brentford

10   Gunnersbury Park

11 Swakeley's, Ickenham

12 Sunbury Court

Church, which he gave to his nephew Carrington. There is, indeed, in existence a copper token of a penny, with the church on one side of it, and a bust in relief of 'David Garrick Esq' on the other. The building is an imposing one : the additions of the mid-nineteenth century were discreet and in keeping. Certainly Garrick had one of the finest entrance porches in Middlesex, with four great brick columns, rusticated, with fine Corinthian capitals and a splendid entablature and pediment. Outside in the square courtyard were two obelisks, one a memorial to Shakespeare, the other to Garrick 'an actor confest, without rival to shine'. Hendon Hall is now a hotel, but the staff were charming and allowed me to see the public rooms and the fine staircase. Two of the rooms have good ceiling paintings, and I heard about the other ceiling painting—a Tiepolo—found in 1948. The painting was probably purchased by Garrick during a stay in Venice; it was subsequently sold. Much of Garrick's times has happily been preserved here.

The Burroughs, near here, was the centre of the Old Hendon village, clustering round the Parish Church. At one end a few of the older houses are left. The pond, once a landmark, has now disappeared, replaced by a pedestrian tunnel under the arterial road: though, as some compensation, there is a fountain nearby. The neo-Georgian library and fire station with the mixed style Town Hall, form a pleasant group. Opposite the well-preserved Daniel Almshouses of 1729 is a large technical college, and beside a little field, the last of the old Church Farm. The Farm House, preserved by the Borough, is now a small and beautifully kept local museum. The ground floor is furnished with authentic pieces, and all the apparatus of an old farm kitchen and sitting room, the upper floors being used for exhibitions. The *Greyhound* next door was the original Church House, but it retains few traces of antiquity.

St. Mary's Church has a prosaic exterior, with a square fifteenth-century tower typical of so many Middlesex churches. But the interior is much more interesting, with a twentieth-century aisle enlarging one of the thirteenth century. Temple Moore, who was responsible, has done the work with discretion and taste. The Norman font and the marble tomb of Sir Jeremy Whichcot, 'the most magnificent floor slab in Middlesex', are admirable, as are the early eighteenth-century monuments of Sir William Rawlinson and Bishop Fowler of Gloucester. My scrutiny of the small brass of John Dower of 1515 was interrupted when I found behind me a charming young woman who, armed with paper and heelball, was about to take a rubbing of it. Learning that I was a comparative stranger to Hendon, she enthusiastically offered to take me round some of the curious tombs in the churchyard. There were many of them, and there was a great deal of ivy and undergrowth. We searched for, but could not find Edward Longmore, the seven foot six 'Herefordshire Colossus' though we were assured that he was still there. But we did find the Gurneys, including Elizabeth with her 22-line epitaph. It is a peaceful churchyard this : I remembered that the footpath opposite led to Sunny Fields and a footpath walk of some miles to Mill Hill—but this is now slashed in two by an arterial road.

Mill Hill East is messy, with a gasometer and a grey and rambling barracks. On the Ridgeway, however, is a real village. Dominating the skyline is the Medical Research Laboratory, a world-famous institution, where, for example, the standard unit of insulin is measured. On the ridge is Littleberries, well concealed in the grey buildings of the Convent of St. Vincent de Paul. The fine window frames indicate the late eighteenth century. For once I had prepared the way, so I rang the bell and asked for Sister Geraldine. However, Sister Clare, who appeared in a few moments was both enthusiastic and knowledgeable. The rear, and older part of the house is panelled, obscurely lit, but rather grand. And the central apartment or 'Gilt Room', which I sought, is splendid, with profuse plaster decorations. The chief feature is an enormous cove to the ceiling with great circular portrait medallions in plaster. They are recognisable from the description as being William III, George I and Caroline of Anspach. But the pictures I was looking for, and the Grinling Gibbons carvings had all disappeared : 'All sold,' said Sister Claire simply, 'we are a charity you know.' And she, knowledgeable as she was, had no idea of who owned the house—and apparently even in 1882, when the place was last described in detail, the owner was not known. Littleberries remains a pleasant mystery.

Mill Hill Ridgeway has all the appearance of a country village, thanks mainly to the School, which has 150 acres of ground on either side of the road. The school buildings, though of varied periods, are far from the 'architectural mess' that one authority calls them. Their mellowed brick and classical pilasters have a certain serenity, while the rear elevation with its six Ionic columns in the portico has great dignity. It is above all the fine trees that give this place its character. It was in Ridgeway House, now incorporated in the school grounds, that the great Quaker Botanist, Peter Collinson, had his nurseries and gardens in the eighteenth century. Here he was visited by Benjamin Franklin and Linnaeus—some Millhillians have it that a few of the present trees were planted by the Swedish botanist. There is no doubt that many of the trees in the school grounds, and nearby, were Collinson's. The governors of the school have preserved much around the Ridgeway. In the grounds of the school, too, is a building known as the 'scriptorium' where James Augustus Henry Murray, a master there from 1870-1885 deposited three tons of paper slips, used in the preparation of the *Oxford English Dictionary*. That the 'greatest lexicographical project of the age' was prepared in this village is an inspiring thought.

There are many picturesque corners to explore around the Ridgeway: Milespit Hill with its Nicoll almshouses and weatherboarded cottages; a modern group of cottages in saw-tooth formation, also weatherboarded, is a genuine effort at conformity; the Victorian St. Paul's Church, built at the instigation of William Wilberforce, 'The Liberator', who lived here for some years; and another delightful group at the top of Hammer's Lane, with Vincett's, a truly Victorian Butcher's shop. At Belmont, now the Junior School, is a curious spiral staircase. It takes three graceful turns up to the top storey, and has a delicate wrought-iron balustrade, and a glass lantern above. The Oval Room is spacious and has a fine plaster ceiling picked out in blue, deep low windows looking out on to lawns, and the countryside. With its fine proportions, it makes a picture of eighteenth-century splendour. The Octagonal Room next door is almost equally fine: the rooms match on each floor and even into the cellars. A fine house this, built in 1765 for Sir Charles Hower, Lord Mayor of London.

The views to the left from Highwood Hill are over the Middlesex plain and out to Harrow—to the left into Hertfordshire. There is a good inn *The Rising Sun* with seventeenth-century brick, Highwood Ash, then Highwood House, brilliant in cream-washed stucco. Now a nursing home, a plaque records the fact that this was the residence of Sir Stamford Raffles. He was a former governor of Java: a naturalist, like Peter Collinson, he founded the Zoological Society. Before him, here lived Lord William Russell: when his arrest was ordered for his complicity in the Rye House Plot in 1684, he is said to have leaped from a second storey window and made for open country.

Daws Lane is urbanised but there is a pleasant public park. The lower part of Hammer's Lane contains the curious little community of the Draper's Cottage Homes—a series of red brick bungalows, laid out in avenues, each with a plaque bearing the name of some great London Store. I recollected that in Hammer's Lane lived one worthy unrecorded by the historians: that great polymath Holbrook Jackson, author of *The Anatomy of Bibliomania*. He was occasionally to be seen in *The Three Hammers*, resting after a country-walk, and talking prodigiously. Here too in Laurel Cottage lived that learned critic and anthologist Daniel George, who in *Tomorrow will be Different* described a country walk round Mill Hill and Arkley in free verse full of wry humour and literary allusion. Another familiar figure in the 'thirties was the white-haired Norman Brett-James, schoolmaster and historian of Mill Hill, Hendon and Middlesex.

Holcombe House (which is open to visitors on Sunday afternoons) has a hall of sheer delight in white, with blue mouldings picked out in gold. The circular staircase is smaller than that of Belmont, but more delicate in style. The house was designed by John Johnson in 1775 for Sir William Anderson, a city alderman, later Lord Mayor of London. The admirable dining room, in green and white, has Grecian figures in raised stucco on its walls. The drawing room (now a library) is more ornate: dolphins and griffons, catkins and acanthus leaves are the decorative *motifs*. The two fine ceiling paintings are attributed to Angelica Kauffmann: they are in her characteristic style, and she was certainly working in Mill Hill in 1776. Holcombe House is used as a guest house for visitors to the Community of St. Mary's Abbey.

Below the Ridgeway and along Watford Way is the aerodrome, Hendon's last large open space. Formerly very extensive, the perimeter has been eaten into by building and the motorway. The old aircraft buildings are decaying, the industry having moved away, and the aerodrome is now used only for occasional training flights. Yet this was once the London Aerodrome, Hendon, and from here some of the pioneers of aviation—Paulhan, Gustav Hamel and Graham-White—made flights in 1910-11. The Handley Page company set up their works on the Cricklewood perimeter in 1912, while the de Havilland company operated later from a smaller airfield at Stag Lane. In 1912 the first Aerial Derby started, and through the years the great names in British aviation, Sopwith, Hawker, Donaldson, have been associated with Hendon. After the First World War the aerodrome was taken over by the new Air Ministry, and a long series of R.A.F. pageants started in 1921. One recollects, in the 'thirties, crowds on the aerodrome and crowds on the nearby Sunny Fields enjoying a free view of the pageant. In the next few years the aerodrome will disappear under 1,800 houses, flats and maisonettes with all the appurtenances of a new community, shops, schools, a library, a club-room and an old people's home.

There will be few here to lament the passing of the aerodrome, or the formerly countrified Colindeep Lane. Close by is the Metropolitan Police College. The wedge of land between the aerodrome and the Edgware Road is covered by the small houses of Colindale and the housing estate at Burnt Oak. Near Colindale Station there is, however, one building of interest, though perhaps only to specialists. In its red brick, with windows rising through three storeys, it resembles a factory: it is the British Museum newspaper repository. Within, the atmosphere is one of calm: one can obtain a temporary ticket for a day's research, with access to vast stocks of newspapers, extensive catalogues and elaborate indexes. In its reading rooms there is little sound save for the turning of yellowed leaves, and the occasional rumble of a trolley as the attendant delivers two or three elephant folios of newspapers, which are propped up on great reading stands.

Burnt Oak, a mile or so from Colindale, is a big housing estate, belonging to the Greater London Council, where over 20,000 people live. It is more humane than most housing estates, having been planned as a whole. But its community buildings are hard to find and there seems to be no centre, unless it be the street market held on Saturdays near the Edgware Road.

Edgware Road, which runs as straight as a ruler from Marble Arch for ten miles to its end, is the old Roman Road—Watling Street. At the Hyde once lived Oliver Goldsmith. Here in 1772 'in search of deep retirement' he came to Hyde Farm, while writing his *History of Animated Nature*. Here in the same year Boswell and Mickle came to visit him. Goldsmith was out and, 'having a curiosity to see his apartment, [I] went in and found curious scraps of descriptions of animals, scrawled upon the wall with a black lead pencil'. But the farm has vanished and there is no trace of Goldsmith except for the names of Goldsmith Avenue and Hyde Crescent.

The tower of Edgware church is fifteenth century, the building heavily restored, and the churchyard crowded with tombstones. The interior is plain and gloomy: apparently the only relic of the past is a brass, very small, on one wall—a babe in swaddling clothes, dated 1557. At Whitchurch the Atkinson almshouses (1828) are neat and well-preserved.

After Whitchurch the Edgware Road rises steadily and becomes Brockley Hill, one of the highest points in Middlesex. At the top is the Royal National Orthopaedic Hospital, with a plaque outside recording the site of ancient potteries. On the right lie the picturesque buildings of the seventeenth-century Brockley Hill Farm. Here is the site of Sulloniacae, a Roman-age settlement. There is a Roman pavement here, and gold coins, rings and urns have been excavated on the site. Here too is open country, on the border of Middlesex, with Harrow to the left, Hendon to the right and Hertfordshire ahead. Open country, but for the Hendon Motorway which cuts a deep scar in the valley, with a complex of roads flying over it. The broken brick arches at the foot of the hill are modern, not Roman, having been part of an Underground railway extension.

Edgwarebury Farm (or house) is on the old maps and is of the seventeenth century. The large half-timbered building is almost too good to be true, with its leaded panes and stained glass, black oak with massive nail heads, a fine porch and two sphinxes at the foot of the steps.

Turning up Canons Drive, we are in Harrow, and in the part of it called Little Stanmore. The remains of a fine gateway form the entrance to this modern housing estate. They were, it is said, the entrance gates to Canons Palace, built by James Brydges, First Duke of Chandos, in 1715, with some of the immense fortune he had accumulated as Paymaster General. It was a fine place: five architects helped to design it, and the park extended to 400 acres. Defoe admired its magnificence: Pope satirised its ostentation in the *Epistle to false taste*. But where is it now? Two of the lakes have been embodied in the modern estate, and very nice they look. Part of the demesne is now playing fields, another part and the former terrace of the Palace, are in the grounds of the North London Collegiate School. A tiny classical temple is the only decorative feature to survive of the original park.

The glory of Canons was brief, for the house was broken up by the second duke in 1747, and portions sold here and there to pay his debts—the great porch at Hendon Hall was part of the original structure. James Brydges lived here in the grandest manner. He was fond of music, and his household orchestra of 30 musicians, led by Pepusch, wrote Defoe, 'entertain him every day at dinner'. His habit of introducing each course at a banquet by a fanfare of trumpets was, perhaps, a trifle ostentatious. But Handel composed anthems for him, and also the oratorio *Hamon and Mordecai*, for a reputed fee of £1,000. The Duke was an ornithologist and a book collector, and a great patron of the arts and music—but not of poetry: this may have prompted Pope's lines

> *In books not authors curious is my Lord*
> *For Locke and Milton 'tis in vain to look*
> *These shelves admit not any modern book*

Both the Dukes led extravagant lives, and many legends have grown up around Canons. But the story about the second Duke trying to buy parcels of land from Edgware to Marylebone, so that he could travel from his town house to his country house on his own land, has now been proved untrue. Chandos House in Marylebone had not been built when Canons was demolished.

The worthy Hallett, a cabinet maker, must have been a more respectable tenant of the Georgian House, now on the site of Canons. But on a visit to the Parish Church I found that the Halletts had passed into history. William Hallett III was married in the church in 1785—and it is he and his bride who are the handsome couple in Gainsborough's 'The Morning Walk', now in the National Gallery.

The parish church of St. Lawrence is reached through Marsh Lane. The tower is sixteenth-century brick, and it is interesting to see how John James or John Price, the architect of 1715, had no inhibitions about placing a modern building next to it. Sober, classical, it is interesting rather than impressive. The grandeur is confined to the interior, the grandeur of Chandos, who endowed it. The Duke's gallery upstairs overlooks the vaulted church. The walls and ceilings are covered by Laguerre's bold frescoes. On either side of the altar are two fine (but uncleaned) paintings by Bellucci, and, above the ducal gallery the same artist's copy of the Raphael *Transfiguration*.

The Chandos Mausoleum to the left of the altar was also being restored when I visited it. I could see most of the great marble tomb of the Duke and his two wives: whether it be by Carpentier or Grinling Gibbons I thought it splendid—even though Nairn says it is 'unfeeling'. And splendid was the impression I took away with me, a feeling of public ceremony rather than religious awe.

CHAPTER FIVE

Kingsbury and Harrow

The traveller in Middlesex is continually beset by the problem of 'getting there', and often the approaches to places of interest are anything but pleasant. The surroundings approaching Brent Cross have a twentieth-century brutality. Brent was at one time a pleasant enough part of Hendon, but now it is dwarfed by a vast motorway bridge, with concrete ramps on either side. Beside them huddle small houses and miniature blocks of flats. On either side are factories, more houses, a sewage farm, a council dump, a lorry park, a grey-hound stadium, a transport café, a railway bridge, and a depot for 'used commercial vehicles'. Here, they say, will arise a drive-in supermarket—this may indeed be an improvement. But, at present, the landscape is an outstanding example of Subtopian horror. I was glad to get into the factory area of the Edgware Road, where a controlled development was more obvious.

Borough boundaries are almost incomprehensible; they can probably be understood best by referring to an old map of the Hundreds of Middlesex, for they scarcely change through the centuries. Here, one travels with Willesden on the left and Hendon on the right; a few hundred yards further on, past the *Welsh Harp*, Hendon takes a great bite out of Willesden across the road; while Kingsbury Road, a half mile on, is in the old borough of Wembley. I once knew a Borough Surveyor whose ambition was to control a 'square borough'. Not even the reorganisation of London's boroughs fulfilled that ambition.

Kingsbury was, a long time ago, a village with a separate existence, and was the King's Manor (or stronghold). It developed into what it is—a dormitory suburb—after 1920. It has no recorded local history, and little connection with national history either. But in Stag Lane it has a connection with the history of aviation. It was here at a small aerodrome in 1920, that the great firm of de Havilland opened their small factory; and from Stag Lane flew the first D. H. Moth, precursor of many great aircraft. There is a good deal about Stag Lane in *Sky Fever*, Geoffrey de Havilland's autobiography: but the amateur of aviation history will find it useless to search for the aerodrome now. The area is a mass of small houses and factories, though there is a Mollison Way and a De Havilland Road.

Up Stag Lane to Roe Green there is a pleasant little park, but no village, with traffic thick on the Kingsbury Road. Still in search of a village, a detour round Buck Lane reveals one of the most curious communities to be seen in North London: a group of castellated houses with a crazy antiquity about them. They are a fascinating collection: Stonegate, Highford and Rochester Courts, all of them battlemented and machicolated, with entrances resembling draw-bridges. Brick, concrete and old stone are mixed in great exuberance, steep eaves, attics and leaded glass complete the parody of antiquity. There are also a few half-timbered houses. Apparently run up by a speculative builder between the wars, these houses seem to indicate that an Englishman's castle can be a home.

But the real village is not to be found here; one turns down Church Lane, for there are farms shown on the map. The Church of St. Andrew repeats the pattern found in other parts of Middlesex, with old and new together: but here there are two complete churches, one ancient, one of the nineteenth century. The old church is very small, with flints embedded in the walls, but there are also some red tiles which are alleged to be Roman. The West side contains stone quoins set in the pre-Conquest 'long and short' manner. Pevsner doubted that the church was built before 1066: but a local historian told me that there was a Roman hypocaust inside. The inside of the church is bleak and bare, and is now used only as a burial chapel. In the little porch of the church there once was a school, founded before 1570, the date Harrow School was founded. Furthermore, the solitary church bell is of the mid-fourteenth century, the oldest bell in Middlesex. Small and unprepossessing, this church is certainly one of the most ancient in Middlesex.

The nineteenth-century St. Andrews is large, with a spire visible for some miles away: it has a curious history, for it was built originally in Wells Street Marylebone, and was erected here, stone by stone, in 1933, when Kingsbury was rapidly developing. The interior is light, airy, rather impressive, with little warmth in it save for the painted panels along the gallery, and some fine Victorian stained glass. But it is not a place to linger in—so I asked the solitary verger who was busy there, for the direction of Blackbird Farm. 'Ah, guv,' he said, 'it's gone long ago.'

And it had—though it was still on a reasonably up-to-date map. There is a new and shiny *Blackbird Inn*, and Blackbird Hill is full of houses. Up the very new looking Salmon Street is some open space, and a gate leading into a field. Preceded by a small girl in gumboots I went in, to find an old barn, with *Bush Farm* crudely chalked on the side. Entering, I was confronted by four teenagers, energetically grooming two ponies. They regarded me with deep suspicion, but admitted that this *was* Bush Farm, and that there were 150 acres, some under grain: but it is mainly used as a riding school. Looking around, plenty of open space can be seen, but no sign of farming activities. This, the last of Kingsbury's farms, seems bound to disappear, just as the village had disappeared some twenty years before.

Kingsbury Circle, which joins the Kenton Road, is the site of the old moot of the Gore Hundred, though there seems nothing to mark the spot. Kenton Road itself, typical of many main roads in London suburbs, is bright, clean, aggressive, with hundreds of shops; on either side of it are two square miles of houses and flats—a typical dormitory suburb. Occasionally there is a building to attract attention, such as a handsome new Catholic Church—but there is nothing to make one stop and admire. At the end of Kenton, comes the large green stretch of Northwick Park, and the grounds of Harrow School, going up Peterborough Hill.

The transition between the bustle of Kenton Road and the quiet of the High Street is like stepping back a century. The High Street is peaceful; there is room to park a car, and room to walk on the pavements; there is little through traffic. The church on the slope dominates everything, just as its spire dominates the Middlesex plain. But the immediate objective is the old school building, approached by a fine red brick terrace.

The old Fourth Form room is the most famous part of Harrow School; and in spite of reading many descriptions of it, I was not in any way disappointed. For this small room, panelled in black oak, with lighter oak above, is a historic place, and the oldest room in the school founded by John Lyon in 1572. At one end is the 'throne' for the headmaster, at the other an armchair for the usher : the boys sat in small stalls on either wall. Above on the lighter oak panelling, beautifully incised, is the official school roll; on the black panelling are the primitive and unofficial carvings of the scholars. This unofficial carving continued for many years until every wall was covered with names and initials, crowded together, sometimes superimposed one on the other. One could spend hours finding names, and connecting them with English history. I found quite a number. 'Robert Peel' 'Aberdeen' 'Temple' (for Lord Palmerston) were all there. Byron cut his name twice, once in a nondescript lower case next to one 'Stedman'; the second, in more elegant capitals, below the name of R. B. Sheridan. The shade of Byron seems to haunt Harrow. Even the telephone exchange was named after him—today it is, more prosaically 822. There are some more rooms on this floor, but no others with these historic associations. The old school is very small, and yet provided enough class rooms for the Harrow of 1820.

Coming out into the High Street on a cold but sunny afternoon and walking the pavements, I experienced none of the 'formidably mid-Victorian character of hearty and confident gloom' that Pevsner felt here. The school buildings are a mixture of various centuries; some of them are overpowering, the chapel hideous. But everything is softened by the 'country town' atmosphere of the place, the idea that the tuck shop and the outfitters had been in use for generations, and by the presence of a few well-kept and restored houses such as Flambards. *The King's Head*, parts of which date from 1533, looked splendid and welcoming, with its signboard and a portrait of Henry VIII. And the boys are as much a feature of the place as the architecture. Strolling around, they looked as if the High Street belonged to them. Some, elegantly clothed, were showing round sisters and friends. The majority wear the huge school scarves, with their straw boaters elegantly tipped over the eyes, cunningly kept in place by an almost invisible piece of elastic. A speckled straw denoted a member of the cricket eleven, crossed arrows on the badge, a monitor. The High Street and its populace were pleasant to survey : it is all very enjoyable, traditional, privileged, and very English indeed.

There are 56 buildings and playing fields belonging to Harrow School—the buildings mainly clustered round High Street and West Street, within an area of half a square mile. Only an old Harrovian would want to see them all. Byron House is interesting, for Matthew Arnold lived there for five years from 1868, admiring the 'old countrified look' of the house. In the Grove, Sheridan lived in some style in 1780, piling up debts. Pie Powder House in West Street is an old municipal building, where the magistrates who regulated Harrow Fair once met. The school Speech Room carries on the tradition of the old Fourth Form Room, for the backs of the chairs have names carved on them, and there are 36 armorial bearings of famous Harrovians, including Sheridan, Lord Rodney, Shaftesbury and Byron. There is also, ironically enough, Anthony Trollope, who was a very grubby day boarder. Dr. Butler, the formidable headmaster, stopped Anthony in the street, asking 'whether it was possible that Harrow School was disgraced by so disreputably dirty a little boy'. So both privilege and ultimate fame play their part in the Harrow School honours.

The parish church of St. Mary, on a slope close to the old school buildings, is ancient. But the fabric, both interior and exterior, has had many restorations. the most drastic being that of Sir Gilbert Scott in 1846. On the way into the churchyard is a bronze plaque recording Lord Shaftesbury's first philanthropic resolution, when he stood near here and saw the 'drunken indecency' of a pauper's funeral. St. Mary's is the most remarkably sited church in Middlesex, built on a hill 300 feet above sea level. Charles II called it 'the visible church'. The views from the tower (which one is allowed to ascend) are magnificent. Some say that 13 counties can be seen. At any rate, Hampstead and Highgate are visible in the East: to the South-East is the vast spread of London with the Victoria Tower, St. Paul's, the Barbican and numerous 'point-blocks' all visible. Due South, Leith Hill and Guildford can be seen on a clear day. On the edge of the churchyard is found Byron's 'favourite spot'—the Peachey tomb—where he sat for hours when he was a boy. Beneath the tomb (restored by his publisher John Murray) is a marble tablet and engraved on it are four lines of the poem *Written beneath an elm in Harrow Churchyard*. Byron was here in 1801: then, he would have had an extensive view of countryside extending to Harrow Weald, Brockley Hill and Elstree. Now there intervene a great sea of grey roofs, countless streets, and the gash of a railway line: in the middle distance a very large green gasometer bears the mysterious word 'No'. For the privileged Byron, life at Harrow was very pleasant: he wrote often of it, and with nostalgia. And I thought of Byron again as I crossed the church porch, for beneath it his daughter Allegra is buried.

The church was originally consecrated in 1094, but little of this date remains except the lowest reaches of the tower. The lancet windows are of the twelfth century, and the splendid roof (made from Harrow trees), with its fine carvings of angels and musicians, is fifteenth century. There is a fine array of brasses, conspicuous among them that of John Lyon, founder of Harrow School, and his wife. The Flaxman monument to Lyon is simple and beautiful. There are two brasses to the Flambards, whose house can be seen in the High Street. And there is a most curious monument to James Edwards, bookseller, collector of 'the rarest specimens biblical and classical of the typographic arts'. There is a staircase leading to a curious room over the porch, called the *Parvise*, which contains a small church museum. St. Mary is a concentrate of Harrow, and of English history. Lanfranc began the building, St. Anselm consecrated it: work was carried on in the thirteenth century by the rector Elias de Dereham, who was responsible for the building of Salisbury

Cathedral. Becket was here in 1170, only 12 days before his martyrdom. Cranmer was here, and surrendered the manor of Harrow to Henry VIII in 1544. The sense of continuity is almost overwhelming. Charles Lamb, who came here often, wrote to Wordsworth about the church's 'instantaneous coolness, and calming almost transforming properties'.

It seemed appropriate, after the historic atmosphere of the church to seek out the manor, so, through the traffic of Station Road I made my way towards Wealdstone and Headstone Manor. There is much concentration of industry, which moved into Wealdstone at the turn of the century. There are many printers, and many famous names: Winsor and Newton, James Powell the glass manufacturers and Kodak are among them. But none of this was too obvious on the way to Headstone, though there is a discreet Kodak building near the entrance to Headstone Park. It is a peaceful place, and was almost deserted on that day. The first sight was the large tithe barn, very well preserved, and said to date from 1600. The Manor House, restored, but with discretion, presented a small two-storeyed frontage —a larger part was visible at the rear. It is surrounded by a brick moat, with ducks paddling around. Much of the building is of the sixteenth and seventeenth centuries, though one or two old bricks bear the date 1501. Wolsey, when rector of Harrow parish, lived here, and is said to have entertained the King here. It was good to see these two historic buildings so well preserved in this delightful park. But this is only one example of Harrow's civic sense, for over one sixth of its 20 square miles is permanent open space. Another example of this instinct for preservation is Pinner Park and village, a mile away.

In Pinner one is nearing the border of Harrow, and not far from Hertfordshire. The roads seemed wider, the houses were elegant and more widely spaced, and the preservation of forest trees very evident. I approached Pinner from behind, for I was looking for Woodhall Towers, 'Tooke's folly', a vast Victorian mansion. But it had disappeared: a new and handsome estate was developing in its grounds. From there Paine's Lane runs into Pinner High Street—a real village street. Pinner for long seems to have led a separate existence to

Harrow, and a fair has been held here since 1386. It still takes place annually near Whitsuntide—'flourishing as never before in its history'. This day there was calm in the High Street, a pleasant contrast to the traffic jam in nearby Bridge Street. Almost all the buildings in the High Street are of some antiquity. The half-timbered *Queen's Head* bears the date 1580—which I thought a little too good to be true. But many of the other houses and shops are Georgian, while Church Farm is seventeenth and eighteenth century. The lanes leading into the High Street also contain some fine old houses, and there are plenty of fine trees. Tucked into the top corner of the street, on a little slope, is the village church: it completes the picture of a village.

The church of St. John the Baptist was consecrated in 1321, and stands on the site of an ancient earthwork. The tower is a typically Middlesex specimen of the fifteenth century. But before going inside there is a large and alarming tomb, towering up to ten feet or so. Known as 'the coffin above the ground', it was erected by Loudon, the Victorian horticulturist, in memory of his parents. John Claudius Loudon, a lowland Scot, bought the lease of Wood Hall Farm in 1807, bringing down his parents from Scotland to help him manage it. He was a man of tremendous industry, writing 32 books, and over 4,000,000 words, on architecture and horticulture. He is credited with the invention of the semi-detached villa, and his 'pattern-books' contained designs by many eminent architects of the time. He introduced the plane tree to London squares, suggested green belts around towns, and was an adept at laying out cemeteries and public parks. He made a fortune, and lost it, dying 'harassed by creditors'. His wife Amelia, author of *The Ladies Flower Garden*, is better known to antiquarian booksellers for the delightful hand-coloured plates in her book. This monument is one of extreme oddity; but I found some more conventional, inside the church. The interior is austere, with touches of scarlet and gold, and a nicely carved modern screen. The oldest things seemed to be three black marble slabs: there is a memorial to J. Z. Holwell, survivor of the Black Hole of Calcutta. And there is an urn to Henry Pye, appointed Poet Laureate to George III in 1790. Poor Pye! his poem in celebration of

13   *The Countess of Derby's tomb, Harefield Church*

NON SARÀ SAN MINERE

A LA DOLCE OMBRA CHE MIA [illegible] DI [illegible]
[illegible] ETERNE E MEL ETERNO LUME
[illegible] IN CHIUDER GLI OCCHI APERSI

IN MEMORY
OF [illegible] MUCH AND LONG LOV'D WIFE
[illegible] LADY NEWDIGATE
[illegible] OF COPPED HALL IN ESSEX ESQ.
[illegible] OF WILLIAM BARON LEMPSTER
[illegible] [illegible] DIED JULY 9. 1774.
[illegible] BARONET WITH MANY TEARS
[illegible] THIS MONUMENT 1775.

the King's birthday with its reference to 'vocal groves and feathered choir' brought jeers from the critics and allusions to 'when the Pye was opened the birds began to sing'. So here is Pye, some way from his native Berkshire. He and Holwell were only two of Pinner's worthies. They include Dean Milman (satirised by Byron), Tilbury (inventor of the carriage), George Gissing and Liza Lehmann; while Horatia, daughter of Horatio Nelson, lived here during the latter part of her life. Her home was in Woodridings, close to Pinner Park.

Harrow is not a place that can be seen in one or two visits: there are too many buildings of interest, and too many historic associations. In Domesday Book it was Herges, a manor of 15,000 acres, belonging to the Archbishop of Canterbury. The name Herges is Saxon, signifying a heathen temple, and the archaeological and place name experts have little doubt that there was some form of temple on the summit of Harrow Hill. Curiously through nearly a thousand years of history Harrow seems to have remained almost intact—for the boundaries of the new London Borough of Harrow are almost exactly the same as those of the old Manor.

Honeypot Lane forms the border between Harrow and Kingsbury. Honeypot has nothing to do with bees, however—it signifies the peculiarly sticky clay of Middlesex; and it is no longer a lane but a broad road, lined on one side by semi-detached houses, on the other by small factories. Anthony Trollope and his family once lived in a farmhouse in the Weald. Julian's Hill in South Harrow was the model of *Orley Farm*. No trace of it now remains, but someone with a sense of the past has named an Orley Farm Road in South Harrow. Trollope has nothing good to say about Harrow, to which he tramped day after day, at first from the Weald, then from Orley Farm—12 miles through the lanes. He was poor, miserable and frustrated: 'I had not only no friends, but was despised by all my companions'. This was in 1830 when Harrow Weald was composed of woods and farmland. Later the Weald was to become the site for mansions of city magnates.

Much of the woods remain: some of the farmhouses have become riding schools or garden centres, some of the mansions have been turned into nursing homes. There is still a private air about Brooks

Common Road and the Common which form two sides of a triangle near the Weald and Stanmore Common. Turning in by *The Hare* into Old Redding (which apparently means a clearing) and passing another country pub *The Case is altered* one comes on the clearing—a belvedere, and a very pleasant one called Grimsdyke View Point. The views are extensive, over woods and fields into Hertfordshire, back, to Harrow-on-the-Hill. Behind is the entrance to Grimsdyke, in some part a public park, but also containing a Norman Shaw mansion, formerly the home of William Schwenk Gilbert.

The grounds are quiet, the path winds through banks of rhododendrons, but soon ends in a five-barred gate, surrounded by minatory notices, all of them meaning 'keep out'. But, having come thus far, I felt a sense of purpose, and went in. Here was the mansion. Built in 1872, it is a fine example of Norman Shaw at his most exuberant, large, rambling, half-timbered, with overhanging gables, tremendous chimneys and leaded glass windows: but obviously deserted, with polythene protection over the windows, and a few naked electric bulbs burning in the interior.

There are 29 acres of ground, once much cultivated, but now somewhat neglected: but the roses are pruned, and daffodils spring up in the leaf-mould underneath the trees. I went through the rose garden and along a footpath. Here was the lake: a summer house was gently falling to pieces; the lake was dark, overgrown with reeds. Gilbert had often said that he would like to die on a summer's day in his own garden. And it was here in this lake that he had died on a summer afternoon in 1911, while teaching two girls to swim. I explored the grounds to the boundary and traced the Dyke that runs through. Then, suddenly I came back into the twentieth century for here stands a 60-foot Post Office tower, bristling with antennae and radar screens.

W. S. Gilbert bought the house in 1890: it had originally been built for Frederick Goodall, the Royal Academician. Gilbert loved this place; he was passionately fond of birds and animals; game birds flourished here, and he would not allow his keepers to shoot even a squirrel. Here he lived the life of a country squire: he took his duties seriously, subscribing to a fund to arrange patrols of the Weald,

78

then infested by footpads. Christmas parties were arranged for the village children. He became a magistrate. There are photographs extant of Gilbert the complete squire in Homburg hat and knicker-bocker suit, and another, very grand, in his uniform as Deputy Lieutenant of Middlesex. He could not have written 'most of his libretti' here, as the Harrow guide states, for only *Utopia Ltd* and *The Grand Duke*, his last collaborations with Sullivan, were written after 1890. But he enjoyed the seclusion of his fine library (into which bullfinches and even deer would penetrate), and the splendour of the music room, with its minstrels gallery. When the great house was sold, dozens of pictures of characters from the Savoy operas were found, and the headman's block and the axe from the *Yeoman of the Guard*.

As late as 1923 Lady Gilbert's outdoor staff had included a bailiff and 14 gardeners. The Christmas parties for village children were still kept up. Grimsdyke, it seems, is to be sold, and may become an hotel. Will Gilbert be commemorated in any way? Surely the residence of a man whose wit gave (and is still giving) pleasure to millions deserves more than a few words in a borough guide.

Down a wide drive nearby is Bentley Priory, which now belongs to the R.A.F. and is built in yellowish stone, massively Victorian, showing no visible sign of Sir John Soane, who made additions to it for the Marquis of Abercorn in 1788. The estate has a long history: there was a Priory here in 1170, which eventually passed to the monks Canterbury, and in 1543 to Archbishop Cranmer. The Priory and its adjacent farm were demolished and the present house started in 1766. In Abercorn's time, the house was famous for its 'fashionable and intellectual gatherings'. Pitt and Wellington stayed here as did Wordsworth, Moore and Scott (who wrote two cantos of *Marmion*). Lord Aberdeen lived here: Queen Adelaide rented the house, and died here in 1849. Now there are Nissen huts on the lawn, a large office block in Ministry of Works style stares at the Victorian build-ing, and the drives are neatly labelled as parking places for officers cars. A superannuated Spitfire sits on another lawn. *Sic transit* Bentley Priory!

Although Harrow Weald is changing, it is changing slowly, and there is still a sense of space and a closeness to countryside. Stanmore's tiny gothic station is soon to disappear—it was once the terminus of a branch line to Harrow and Wealdstone, along which ran the 'Stanmore Rattler'. The line, built in 1890, is said to have transformed Stanmore from an agricultural village into a suburb. But it is a suburb well cared for, spacious, with many forest trees around. Clement Attlee lived here for 14 years until 1945, when his responsibilities brought him another house to live in. He writes in his autobiography of how restful the place was then. Nobody whom I asked knew where Heywood, his house, could be, and there is no Attlee Drive in Stanmore.

The most picturesque part of the old village is round the parish church of St. John in Church Road. Here is an eighteenth-century rectory, a barn converted into cottages, and the old Church House— and there is a twentieth-century 'Manor House' which has mellowed enough to seem almost of the right period. The churchyard, like others in Middlesex, exhibits old and new together; the ruined red brick tower of 1632, and the Victorian church which replaced the old one. Coming up the path, I was looking for a tomb surmounted by a white angel—and there it was, on its base, the word 'Mackintosh'; the real inscription was on a horizontal slab—this was the grave of W. S. Gilbert.

The interior is characterised by Nairn as 'mean-spirited'. I, like Pevsner, admired it; so much of the old had been preserved. There is a fine monument to Sir John Wolstenholme, the founder of the church. Merchant adventurer, he was a founder of both the East India and Virginia Companies. There was John Burnell of the Clothworkers Company, his monument kept in good trim by the company. And, after a search I found Lord Aberdeen, recumbent in semi-darkness on the west wall: here was another old Harrovian: statesman, antiquarian—the 'travelled thane' of Byron's *English Bards and Scotch Reviewers*. There is a fine font bearing the Wolstenholme arms, and a hideous one given to the church by Queen Adelaide.

Harrow must certainly be a pleasant place to live in, but like many suburbs with great stretches of streets, it sometimes seems lonely. Kenton in particular is an easy place to get lost in: streets are like a maze. There are plenty of modern churches, but only one that invited entry—St. Alban's Church in North Harrow, one of A. W. Kenyon's finest, which has a noble simplicity in its vaulted interior, lofty, white and cool. There are fine schools, in Middlesex County Council's best style. There is a civic pride in the place, with open spaces jealously preserved: and efforts to build reservoirs at Harrow-on-the-Hill are being stoutly resisted.

CHAPTER SIX

Around the Brent

The Brent is the largest natural river of Middlesex, rising south-west of Chipping Barnet and flowing some 20 miles into the Thames at Brentford. It runs through Hendon roughly parallel to the North Circular Road, passing under Edgware Road. It is dammed to form the Welsh Harp. It then winds through Neasden, Acton and Ealing, to Southall (where it forms part of the Grand Union Canal) and finally comes into the Thames. For the greater part of the way it is invisible to the passer by, swallowed up in its passage by houses, factories, railways and sidings. The name Brent is an ancient one: the learned Ekwall (foremost authority on river names) connects it with the goddess Brigantia—'a clear instance of river names pointing to river worship'. Far from worshipful today, the Brent is no longer the clear stream whose 'cool waves in limpid currents stray', as Byron write: it is grey, sour and polluted, and no longer fishable except by the most optimistic. Brent and the canal cross and intermix through the boroughs of Willesden, Wembley and Acton.

The most hopeful approach to Wembley is through the half rural scene of the Welsh Harp, an artificial lake originally made to provide water for the Regent's Canal. It is a considerable expanse, 350 acres in all, and round its border are sports and recreation grounds. In Victorian times it was celebrated for pigeon-shooting and there was a notoriously rough and rowdy race course there, 'low, vulgar and commonplace to a degree', wrote Walford, 'and utterly ignored by the committees who arrange the details of Epsom and Ascot'. Nowadays it is more sedate. On sunny Spring days there is a sparkle about the Harp, with small sailing boats bobbing around, and youngsters hopefully fishing from the banks. In Summer there are speed boat races, firework displays, and international regattas. The grass banks are scrubby with a few trees and bushes: the Welsh Harp is no longer a bird sanctuary; but in spite of the hubbub of the Edgware and North Circular roads many birds live and breed there. It is one of the watching points of the London Natural History Society. Such rare species as dunlin, grebe and blackcaps have been seen: kestrels have bred, and gadwall, smew and mute swans are there in winter. Up to a few years ago a stately heron from the Welsh Harp was seen at 6.30 every evening over Crouch End Broadway, on its way to roost at Tottenham Marshes.

Cool Oak Lane wanders pleasantly along the banks of the Harp: nurseries and sports grounds replace the pastures that once were there, and the oaks have gone. At the top of the rise there is a community of neat bungalows that has one of the most pleasant views in these parts, across fields and water, with not a factory in sight, and free of traffic. Only a few yards on, and one comes to Forty Lane and Wembley Town Hall. The building is fortress-like: its brick-work is magnificent, but the place looks unwelcoming. It has, how-ever, an unusually spacious foyer and an excellent municipal hall; everything seems to happen here: symphony concerts, wrestling, amateur drama. This town hall, surely badly placed for Wembley, is even more off centre for the new borough of Brent, of which Wembley is a part. There is an attractive and very busy branch lib-rary, but the staff were not too busy to find a local history for me, which was issued with the minimum of fuss, although I was a stranger. Opposite the Town Hall is rising an uncompromising block of con-crete flats with great semi-circular bastions at each corner—the bastions are strictly functional, for they are refuse chutes. There are to be 2,000 dwellings in this vast Chalk Hill scheme—a typical ex-ample of soulless planning—'convenient filing cabinets for the work-ing classes'. They exemplify the uneasy marriage between the prosperous middle-class Wembley and the industrialised (and decay-ing) Willesden in the borough of Brent.

This part of Wembley is dominated by the Stadium and the Arena, the two buildings that have made the name Wembley the best-known of any Middlesex suburb. The Stadium with its four domed towers is one of the few remaining buildings of the British Empire Exhibition of 1924. Its style reminds one of Lutyens' New Delhi. It holds 120,000 people; on its meticulously tended football pitch countless Cup Final battles have been fought. The Arena and Swimming Pool, of 1934, is one of Sir Owen William's more notable constructions, its massive sides resembling an up-ended pack of gigantic concrete playing cards. The approaches are on the scale of the buildings, with giant coach parks; but how such vast numbers get out of and into the small Wembley Park tube station is a mystery. On its busy days this part of Wembley is the centre of a traffic whirlpool, with its turbulence extending for miles around. On a quiet day it looks bleak and melancholy. Some of the other buildings remaining from the exhibition have been taken over as factories: others, newer, are concrete and glass slabs, mostly dull. The streets round this centre are bewildering in their profusion of signs—and once out of it the motorist gets wedged in the traffic jam of Wembley High Street, full of traffic signs, pedestrian crossings, and shoppers.

Wembley is definitely of the twentieth century. Its population in 1901 was about 4,500: in 50 years it had increased to 131,000, the greater part of this being from 1924, the date of the British Empire Exhibition. Residential Wembley is a complex series of avenues, crescents, ways, and gardens ('street' and 'road' are seldom used), many of them with neat grass borders and flowering trees. There are hundreds of semi-detached houses with fresh paint, well-tended gardens, and every appearance of prosperity. The stranger in town, seeking directions, has to rely on the goodwill of the residents. I found plenty of it: but nobody seemed to know that Wembley had any history. Quartering avenue after avenue in search of Lyon's Farm proved to be a vain search: it has now vanished, built over. Yet this was the farm where John Lyon, the founder of Harrow, had lived. There are indeed two places named 'Lyon' in Wembley, but far from this area of Barn Hill, and my supposition that the farm had gone was later confirmed by the local archivist. But the name 'Uxenden' proved to be more rewarding, for it led to Barn Hill Recreation ground. It was an open space rather than a park, with a few paths in the grass; but on the hill was a line of poplars which must have led to a house. This had been Uxenden Manor, in the sixteenth century the residence of the Catholic family of Bellamy. And it was here, in 1586, that Anthony Babington and his friends found their final refuge after their plot to kill Queen Elizabeth was discovered. Babington, Ballard and their associates were a singularly stupid set of conspirators, toasting the success of their enterprise in London taverns. They were seized on Walsingham's orders, put in the Tower, and afterwards executed 'with the utmost barbarity'. Uxenden Manor has gone, and there is nothing to mark the spot. Here is only a plot of grass, a triangulation point and some good views over to Harrow and Central London. But there is something to be said for preservation of these open spaces in Middlesex. I found many times that there was some history attached to them.

Sudbury, once a manor of Harrow, is the older part of Wembley and has a longer history: but little of it is visible today. Barnham Park is charming, presented to the borough by one of its noted residents; but the Georgian mansion that went with it has disappeared. The only remains are some old walls and a fine matured garden. A Victorian house in the park houses a branch library which has an interesting collection of local material. Sudbury Court Road nearby does contain one seventeenth-century house, but it is nondescript and decaying. Hillside Farm has been partially built over; yet it must have been in this area where Trollope's father rented the farm he managed so badly, and where Anthony lived. This part of Wembley has grown fast, with little of its antiquity preserved. There is said to be one farm building, Hundred Elms, still occupied, but it is impossible to find. The only two modern buildings worthy of any respect are Charles Holden's two tube stations at Sudbury Town and Sudbury Hill, the former remarkable for its lofty booking hall, and its austere design.

Wembley history, therefore, is scarcely visible to the visitor. There is nothing of note in its parish church; but in its graveyard there is one stone to the boroughs' most eminent worthy: Sir William Perkin, the greatest organic chemist of his time. In 1853 at the age of 15 he entered the Royal College of Chemistry, becoming a pupil of the famous Hoffmann. By the age of 18, he had become Hoffmann's honorary research assistant, and was experimenting in a rough laboratory in his home at Sudbury. Working with his brother on aniline compounds, he discovered the first completely fast mauve dye. It was enthusiastically received by Pullar's of Perth. Within a few months Perkin had opened a small factory at Greenford, and was making dyes in quantity. 'A rage for your colour has set in among that all-powerful class of the community—the ladies,' wrote Pullar; 'if they once take a mania for it and you can supply the demand, your fame and fortune are made.' Mauve was the favourite colour of Queen Victoria—and the fortune was made: Perkin retired at the age of 35 to The Chestnuts, Sudbury. There he devoted himself to research in pure chemistry, to good works and to chamber music. Perkin, a shy and retiring man, received many distinctions, and was knighted in 1906, the jubilee of his discovery. The whole of his story has been well told by J. G. Crowther. Today even The Chestnuts has disappeared, and nothing of Perkin remains except the tombstone.

From Wembley Park down to Alperton there is an industrial belt, with a tangle of railway lines round Neasden and the North Circular Road. The Brent, winding its way through the pleasant Tolkyngton recreation ground, does little to mitigate the harshness of the industrial landscape. The river disappears beneath the Grand Union Canal, which is carried on a viaduct over the North Circular Road. The harried motorist rushing down the road has no time to notice the arms of Middlesex on the viaduct; or to look at the factories—the names they bear are more distinguished than their architecture.

Willesden has a longer history than Wembley: its Anglo-Saxon name, Wellesdune, indicating the hill of the spring. The name Willesden appears in Domesday Book, and the place was wholly church-owned by St. Paul's under ninth-century charter. The total area of Willesden today is almost the same as in mediaeval times. Once rich agricultural land supplying London with food, it is now overbuilt, with many factories: most of its development taking place in the last 50 years of the nineteenth century. Even the official guide to the borough, where one would expect the best aspect to be put on things, laments 'the old houses swept away in the flood of uncontrolled development'. Its historian, J. T. Gillett, writes of it as a 'vast transit camp, with few of its population having any roots in the place.' Willesden is a place of contrasts, varying from the sedate respectability of Cricklewood to the seedy atmosphere of Kilburn and the teeming industry round its famous junction.

Neasden, its suburb near the Welsh Harp, gives a foretaste of the mixture of housing and industry. Here the borough is crossed by five sets of railway lines, which are spanned by a vast steel bridge. Once through the shopping centre there are terraces of houses and flats, with one late eighteenth-century house—The Grange—conspicuous among them. The house was to be preserved, and might have become a museum and arts centre: but it, too, is threatened by a scheme for an underpass under the North Circular road. Turning the corner by the Grange, two vast cooling towers of a power station dominate the shallow valley of Neasden; and these, with two more farther west, seem to cut the borough in half. In the nearby Coles Green Road, almost hidden among small shops and factories, is the boroughs' second oldest building, Oxgate Farm, the only remnant of Willesden's agricultural past. About 1600, says one authority, but a wooden signboard round the side of the farmhouse boldly announces '1483'. One can only guess: the irregular tiled roof, the blackened beams round the door seem authentic; elsewhere there has been much restoration. A recent refurbishing yielded, behind a daub and wattle wall, an Elizabethan bottle and a coin of the same period. So this tiny building is probably sixteenth century. It is still occupied and will be preserved.

The district to the right of the Edgware Road is Cricklewood.

> *... Midland, bound for Cricklewood*
> *Puffed its sulphur to the sunset where that*
> *Land of laundries stood*

wrote Betjeman. Now the diesel trains slip by more silently, and most of the laundries have gone. But Cricklewood and South Acton (known as 'Soapsud Island') were once laundering centres. There were brickworks in the area, brickmaking was a seasonal occupation, and brickmakers married laundresses who earned money for the family in the idle months. Now the brickworks have vanished, and there is a varied fringe of factories round Cricklewood's border. It is a staid place, well laid out, with plenty of street trees—though it scarcely is on garden city lines, as one writer suggests. The steep streets lead up to its major open space of a hundred acres, Gladstone Park. And on its top is a building in typical Post-Office Georgian, the Research Station, its radio masts visible for miles around. The tea pavilion in the park was formerly a suburban retreat for Lord Aberdeen. The great W. E. Gladstone made frequent visits here from 1882-1896. A plaque on the front of the pavilion commemorates these visits, but the plaque is half obliterated, the building looks shabby—and the tea is indifferent. To find other traces of Gladstone one has to go to the parish church, and to Willesden High Road.

From *The Crown* in Cricklewood, down Chichele Road and Walm Lane a neatly laid out pattern of streets appears on either side, but little of interest except the tall tower to St. Gabriel's Church, famous for its acoustics; a number of recordings have been made there. Coming down into Willesden High Road the houses seem to shrink, and the streets to narrow. The parish church, St. Mary, is set apart on a little green Churchyard. Heavily restored in the nineteenth century, its interest is concealed by a rather dull exterior. Just in front of the porch is the prominent tomb of Charles Reade, author of *The Cloister and the Hearth*. And near him lies his platonic friend Laura Seymour, the actress, who kept house for him for 25 years until 1879: the inscription on the tomb is 'Her face was sunshine, her voice was melody, and her heart was sympathy'.

The church tower is square and low, in a typical Middlesex style. The oldest parts of the church are of the thirteenth and fourteenth centuries, though its records go back to 1181. St. Mary's was once famous for its image, 'The Black Virgin of Willesden', which was supposed to have miraculous properties; and, like the Mus Well, it became a place of pilgrimage. But the fairs and festivities attached to the pilgrimages became a scandal and finally in 1538, by Thomas Cromwell's motion 'all the notable images unto which were made anie especial pilgrimage and offerings were utterlie taken away and burnt at Chelsea by the Lord Privie Seal'. So Willesden's Virgin has gone. But much else has been rescued and preserved: there is a fine series of brasses, the earliest dating from 1492; the font is of the twelfth century; the font in the chapel, Elizabethan. The memorials of the seventeenth century reveal a connection of the Franklyns of Willesden with the Mint, and of Henry Finch, 'last survivor of the company of Moneyers'. A Victorian brass tablet records that W. E. Gladstone was a communicant here from 1882-1894. A recent tablet records the last restoration of the church in 1946 and the contributions made by some of the great industrial firms of the borough—familiar names such as McVitie, Heinz and Guinness. And on the massive oak door is a notice recording that the holes in it were made by Cromwellian bullets. Thus it seems that most of Willesden's history is summarised in its church.

Church Road leads into Harlesden and Willesden Junction. Industrial squalor predominates here: the housing is crowded, the shops mean, and the streets littered. The railway junction (which one thinks of in connection with Willesden) is a maze of lines and platforms—but only one platform is within the borough of Willesden. The industrial landscape round the Grand Union Canal is grim: the towpath is broken and neglected, with patches of scrubby grass. The canal itself is grey-green and greasy, with little traffic of barges. There are two more enormous cooling towers and a power station. Alongside the canal is a lorry graveyard, piled with chassis, cabs, brake drums and old wheels. The only note of colour is the brash new Freightliner Station, painted a bright yellow: and industrial litter continues for over a mile of towpath.

Here, and in Kensal Rise and Kilburn, is the border with metropolitan London. In Kilburn High Road the *Bell* tavern marks the site of the mediaeval Priory, while the station is on the site of the medicinal spring of Kilburn Wells; the latter is marked by a plaque on the nearby Barclay's Bank. Kilburn Grange has vanished, being replaced by one of the largest cinemas in the suburbs. This is a dreary stretch of road, but it must once have been pleasantly rural. Julius Caesar Ibbetson lived near here and painted a few pictures of Kilburn and Willesden. William Harrison Ainsworth lived in The Elms and the Manor House at Kensal Green from 1834 to 1853. He wrote some of his best novels here, including *Rookwood*, *Windsor Castle* and *Old St. Paul's*. In *Jack Sheppard* he placed his hero in Willesden, where he never was—and thus started a number of legends. But all this was a long time ago, and it takes a good deal of imagination to bring back any charm to this seedy district. It is, however, slowly being improved by municipal housing, some of it intelligently planned and good-looking. To immigrants from Ireland, Kilburn must be a haven. Many of them live here, boarding with Irish families. Their presence is obvious in the piles of Irish newspapers seen in the shops. There are pubs used almost exclusively by Irishmen. There are Gaelic clubs, and in Kilburn High Road is the Emerald Agency, where 6,000 immigrants are found employment every year. There is, even, rumoured to be a Hurling club in existence.

The best municipal planning is seen in Willesden's parks. Queen's Park, near the Kilburn High Road, softens the severity of this district with its 30 acres of green. It was the grounds of a famous football club—The Rangers—and was purchased by the City of London in 1887. It was developed with excellent taste, provided with many trees, not only the familiar limes, chestnuts and sycamores, but other rarer varieties. Standing in its centre today, the stolid Victorian houses that surround the park can just be seen through a belt of mature trees. The shrubberies are well arranged, there is a miniature golf course, and a charming Victorian bandstand. Although there have been complaints about 'unplanned' felling of trees, Queen's Park is still a delightful place to come across from the brick wilderness of Kilburn. The most elegant of Willesden's open spaces, however, is Roundwood Park some two miles away. In the Spring it is remarkable for its beds of massed tulips in brilliant colours, provided 200 to a bed. A delightful rockery and pool is near the entrance, the paths wind gently up a hill, and there is plenty of grass to walk on. And on top of the hill there are views for miles around, not only of the cooling towers, but over to Wembley, Kingsbury and Harrow.

Willesden's western border with Acton is industrial, but industry planned and regulated—the massive complex of Park Royal. It is traversed by two wide roads. Coronation Avenue and Twyford

Abbey, and from them and their offshoots are avenue after avenue of factories large and small, tidy, all seemingly smokeless, manufacturing everything from biscuits to electrical gear. Car parks, and container wagons are everywhere: during the week Park Royal is no place for a visitor. I went there on a Saturday when everything was quiet. Architecturally there is little to remark on, except that the place is orderly and does not assault the eye. One building only stands out: the Guinness Brewery, designed by Giles Gilbert Scott in 1936, and certainly the only architectural masterpiece in Willesden. The main building is of four great blocks of brickwork, with apertures rather than windows, solid and impressive. There are many smaller buildings, all well composed into a harmonious whole, set in green lawns. There are sports clubs and homes for workmen and senior staff. This is an orderly and well-organised factory, with architects on the staff who arrange any alterations to buildings. Only brewing is done here and a fleet of a hundred tankers, carrying 2,500 gallons at a time, take the ale out to be bottled elsewhere. Most of this I learned from a genial guard seated in a kiosk at the gate: on his table were arranged three bottles of Guinness—these, he explained were the free daily ration for each employee—but they had to be consumed on the premises. Parties of visitors to the factory are allowed the same privilege. Guinness are a remarkable firm in their public relations. They had contributed to the cost of restoration of Willesden church; they were the sponsors of the annual *Guinness Book of Records*; one thinks also of their brilliant advertising, and the remarkable Iveagh collection at Kenwood. And they preserve the last vestiges of rural Willesden in the nearby Twyford Abbey, a nursing home of the Catholic Order of Alexian Brothers. Its Victorian gothic building of 1808 is on the site of an old manor house, and is kept in the same impeccable condition as the other Guinness properties. The motorist near the North Circular Road may be startled by a 'cattle crossing' notice; but there are cattle in the fields, there is a farm and the remnants of the ancient village of Twyford.

In Park Royal, Willesden merges with the neighbouring borough of Acton, and the visitor cannot distinguish one from the other.

The great arterial road, Western Avenue, begins in Acton, sweeping through Ealing and continuing to the Middlesex border at Uxbridge, and is, for much of its length, fringed with factories. In the first stage of the avenue is Wales Farm Road: on a signal box on the railway line is the sign 'Acton Wells'. They are both a reminder that Acton once possessed an eighteenth-century spa. The Wells were in Old Oak Lane and flourished between 1750-1790. It is difficult to realise that these nondescript streets were once a fashionable resort 'thronged with valetudinarian and idle inmates'. The Assembly Rooms and the pleasant villas that were built near the Wells have all vanished, as have most of Acton's old buildings, and only street names remain to remind us of its worthies and its history. Some places have gone without trace. Where, for instance was Sir Robert Poyntz' Park at Acton? John Aubrey records that Sir Walter Raleigh 'standing in a stand at Sir Robert Poyntz' ... took a pipe of tabacco, which made the ladies quitt it till he had done'. The records do not show the park, nor could I find where, or why, Earl Ferrars (who lived in Muswell Hill) had sent on his coach and six after his execution at Tyburn. These may be legends, of course: but they indicate that Acton had a history, though it is well concealed.

As usual, history has to be sought in the parish church, St. Mary's, off the High Street. The modern buildings in the High Street are imposing enough, with a large town hall, public baths and library grouped together. St. Mary's Church of 1875 is rather hemmed in and spoilt by its surroundings. Many of the memorials from the old church have been preserved. There is one very fine brass of 1558— Humphrey Cavell, kneeling before a prayer desk. The 1698 monument to William Aldridge reveals that he lived to the extraordinary age of 115. The flagstaff from the old church is an enormous acorn, signifying that 'Oaktown' was in the centre of a forest. But the most interesting tablets show Acton's connection with Cromwellian times. There are memorials to the wives of Francis Rous and Philip Skippon. Rous was a provost of Eton, and a member of the Protector's Parliament. Skippon was commander of the London Militia in 1648, and Cromwell's major-general. He was a man of some conscience, and declined to be a judge at the trial of Charles I. Nevertheless, his name

has been crossed off the parish register, and the word 'Traytor' substituted. Two stone effigies on the west doorway commemorate Richard Baxter, theologian, and Sir Matthew Hale, Lord Chief Justice. Baxter, a strong Presbyterian, lived in Acton in 1663, preaching in his own house, opposite the church door. Hale was subsequently the tenant of the house: he was, writes Aubrey, 'not only just, but wonderfully charitable and open-handed and did not sound a trumpet neither, as hypocrites doe'. Baxter and Hale became close friends. 'We were oft together and almost all our discourse was philosophical', wrote Baxter.

Acton must have been a stronghold of the Puritans. It was here in 1651 that the Lord Mayor of London and his aldermen met Oliver Cromwell after the battle of Worcester, handing him a laudatory address. Essex and Warwick had their headquarters in Acton during the Civil War. In South Acton near Turnham Green occurred one of the decisive actions of the war, when the Royalists, flushed with their looting of Brentford were confronted by 24,000 men of the trained bands. There was a brisk Cavalry action: but the bands stood firm, and the Royalists retreated. This 'fight', rather than battle, was a turning point in the conflict, and is commemorated by a tablet in the church at Bedford Park, which laments the 600 Royalist dead.

Most of Acton's history is concealed from the visitor: there is a complete absence of plaques indicating any historic site or street; much of it is unplanned, with small factories in the most unexpected places. Many of its partly industrial areas are as dreary as any Runcorn or Widnes. The area round Acton Central station is typically seedy: yet coming into East Churchfield Road the fine porch and colonnade of the Goldsmith's Almshouses shine out like a good deed in a naughty world. There are fine lawns, and two notable cedar trees set off the building. An obelisk is opposite, erected in memory of the Earl of Derwentwater, who was executed for his part in the Jacobite rebellion of 1715. 'On account of his youth and popular manner his death excited general compassion', we are told. His house was near here in Derwentwater Road, and its main gates were never opened again after his execution. Here too is one of Acton's few open spaces: Acton Park and sports ground—an unexpected and welcome glimpse of green in the middle of acres of brick. Two of Acton's best modern buildings are near here. East Acton Court in the lane of that name is an elegantly designed block of flats by G. A. Jellicoe, while in Old Oak Lane is one of Edward Maufe's finest churches, St. Saviour's.

In fact, the majority of Acton's most interesting buildings are in the half of a square mile centring on the Town Hall: and it is here that Berrymead Priory, a house full of associations, is to be found. It is not easy to find: Salisbury Street is narrow, and was full of lorries the day I visited it: in fact the Priory is part of the premises of Nevill's Bread Factory. The Priory was of the sixteenth century, and it was, according to the records a 'religious house containing upwards of forty nuns'. But it has been rebuilt more than once, and was owned by the Duke of Kingston in George II's reign. The present early nineteenth-century building, battlemented, with all the appearance of a mediaeval castle, was built for a Colonel Clutton in 1802. It has had many tenants since then: it was once a Constitutional Club, and is now used by the bread manufacturers as a place of recreation for their employees. On entering one is confronted by a large Victorian 'baronial hall' extending to two storeys, complete with beamed roof, massive staircase and gallery. It is said that some of this hall may be part of the original structure: certainly the heads on the corbels are older than the nineteenth century; the stag's heads high on the wall are probably the whim of some Victorian owner, and make the place look like a stage-set. The basement rooms have walls three or four feet thick, and are undoubtedly part of the old Priory. The ground-floor rooms have a curious arched structure: they are spacious, but full of tables, chairs and coffee-machines, with notices forbidding gambling. Upstairs, one may see more of what the Victorian mansion was like. The billiard room has more massive arches and deep-window embrasures. The drawing room contains a secret panel and a hiding hole: yet this may be another Victorian caprice, and there are other rooms, used as offices and board rooms, which the visitor cannot see. This is a fascinating building, some of it sham, some of it authentic. Here Edward Bulwer Lytton (traces of whom are to be found in many places in Middlesex) lived in 1836, the year after he had written *Rienzi*, and the year of his legal separation from his wife, who pursued him with lawsuits thereafter. Lola Montez, the dancer, lived here in 1849 after her banishment from Bavaria. There is nothing in the building to record the presence of either of them, though most of this information may be found in the local archives of the public library. But Acton, like many other places in Middlesex is stingy in its provision of plaques on its notable buildings, whereas the visitor in central London can find them everywhere.

Thus there is only a street sign to indicate Bedford Park. On Acton's border with Chiswick, a garden suburb founded in 1875 by Jonathan Carr to provide 'artistically designed family houses at moderate rents for professional or business men'. The land belonged to the Russell family, and Carr's first action was to preserve the maximum number of trees on the estate; and they are preserved still. Bedford Park has not the spaciousness or the overall sense of planning of the Hampstead Garden Suburb, but it was 25 years earlier, and long before Ebenezer Howard gave his ideas on town planning. Norman Shaw was the chief architect, and he was at his exuberant best in the suburb's two principal buildings, the Church of St. Michael and All Angel's, and the *Tabard*. The Inn, with its great porch, timbering and gables was to be copied and vulgarised by brewers for 50 years, and was to be the prototype for hundreds of 'Olde Englyshe' pubs—but the *Tabard*, with its intricate detailing, still retains much of its charm. St. Michael's is inimitable, with its vast gabled frontage and its barn-like interior with most of its structure exposed. The decoration inside exhibits the influence of the pre-Raphaelites, and the modern additions are all in keeping with Shaw's original ideas. In the porch, there is a bronze plaque commemorating the Battle of Turnham Green with 'six hundred of Prince Rupert's cavaliers dead'.

The suburb itself is a curious complex place of winding streets and dead ends. The style of the houses was at first referred to as 'Queen Anne', but it is much earlier than that: steep gables, overhanging eaves and unusual porches abound. W. B. Yeats, who lived here for seven years, wrote of its 'crooked ostentatiously picturesque streets'.

A contemporary number of the *St. James' Gazette* called it 'a place where men may lead a correct, chaste and aesthetical existence'. G. K. Chesterton was to poke fun at it in his fantasia *The Man Who was Thursday*. 'The suburb of Saffron Park was built of bright red brick throughout: its skyline was fantastic, and its plan was wild. Although its pretensions to be an intellectual centre were a little vague, its pretensions to be a pleasant place were indisputable'. Jack Yeats lived here; so did Lucien Pissarro at 62 Queen Anne's Gardens; Camille, his father, painted several pictures of the district when he stayed there in 1897. Today Bedford Park has still an air of decorum and aestheticism: it is beautifully kept, and has a Bedford Park Society which is determined to protect its larger houses from the blight of multiple occupation. It is, as Michelin would say, 'worth the detour'.

CHAPTER SEVEN

Ealing and its Villages

The eastern border of Ealing is Park Royal, with the industry of Willesden and Acton; to the south is Hounslow, and a border formed by the Brent and Grand Union Canal; while eastwards Ealing stretches out into the countryside and the new London borough of Hillingdon. Ealing was a favourite out-of-town resort in the eighteenth century; after 1838, when the Great Western Railway built a station there, it grew rapidly, and it became the first Middlesex borough in 1901. It is a good example of a small town developing from a series of villages: development unplanned as a whole, but discreet, respectable, mostly middle class. Several of the larger housing estates have been planned to some effect, with wide avenues and many trees. Today the villages from which Ealing expanded—Hanwell, Greenford, Perivale and Northolt—are still recognisable as such, with their parish churches and village greens. Industry (and there is plenty of it) is mostly centred on Western Avenue. There seem to be no slums; while the borough's boast that she was 'Queen of the Suburbs' has still some validity. These is still a spacious air about the place: an unusual and pleasant feature is the large number of green spaces between the houses; there are 51 of them on the map; and whether they are commons, parks, golf courses, sports grounds or even cemeteries they are pleasant to come upon, and seldom more than half a mile apart. Some, like those in Perivale and Greenford, are of considerable size; and for good measure there is the 180 acres of Gunnersbury Park, just outside the border, but maintained jointly by the boroughs of Ealing and Hounslow.

The approach to Ealing is through Hanger Lane, once a country lane, where Charles Dibden lived and wrote many of his best sea songs; but this was in the late eighteenth century. Now Hanger Lane is a wide avenue, an extension of the North Circular Road; but not wide enough for the enormous motor traffic using it, for at certain times of the day it is full of exasperated motorists. The first mile or so of Hanger Lane is a hill and from the rise there are views to Wembley and Harrow. On either side lies the handsome Hanger Hill housing estate, one side of it arranged in a series of elegant semi-circular drives, the other in a maze-like arrangement of roads, complete with sports-grounds, park and schools. Everything is neat, with tidy gardens, well-kept borders and bright paint. On the left side the estate culminates in Queen's Drive, half a mile of timber-framed houses and flats, immaculate in cream and black; they are all so obviously of the twentieth century that the effect is almost comic. On the right side is Ealing Village, screened by a high wall, with its own lodge (and telephone number); very exclusive indeed: the visitor may well feel he is trespassing.

Past tree-lined Ealing Common is Gunnersbury Avenue, and the park, one of the most remarkable in outer London and one of the least frequented, for few motorists make the effort to get into Pope's Lane and its entrance. The park is spacious, splendidly laid out, and contains five buildings scheduled for preservation as 'historic'. The original Gunnersbury House has now vanished, demolished in 1801. Its most famous tenant was the Princess Amelia Sophia Eleanora, the daughter of George II, who lived here from 1763-1786. She did not marry, retired from the court and entertained all the neighbouring celebrities, including Horace Walpole, who was there every week; he wrote a birthday ode for the princess. The house has gone, but the remarkable battlemented 'Princess Amelia's bath house' remains to puzzle the antiquarians, with its alternative titles of 'dairy', 'cottage', or 'chapel'; whatever it was, it is highly picturesque today, full of nooks and crannies, secluded gardens and stone walks. The two mansions which replaced the original house, called 'Gunnersbury House' and 'Gunnersbury Park Mansion', ultimately came into the possession of the Rothschild family. Lord Nathan Rothschild, the first Jewish Member of Parliament, lived here from 1836, altering and improving the estate. One mansion housed the family, the other his guests. The great Sydney Smirke made alterations to the mansion, John Claudius Loudon improved the entrance and suggested new plantings of trees. Leopold de Rothschild succeeded his father as owner of Gunnersbury and after his death the whole estate was bought for public ownership.

The result of some 200 years of care and improvement coupled with typical Rothschild good taste, have resulted in this park, embellished with splendid trees, full of vistas and of curiosities: in fact equal to some more famous 'stately homes' open to the public. There is a delightful Gothic folly near Potomac pond, a classic temple, flower beds, rockeries, water gardens. Some of the floral curiosities, such as the blue water lilies, may have gone, but, in season, there is a magnificent red camelia, well protected, trained against the walls of the garden pavilion. For once (a necessity lacking in many parks) one can sit in the open near a well-kept refreshment pavilion, enjoy some tea and look over green lawns.

The mansion itself is now a museum of local history, industry and crafts. The rooms are large, lofty and well kept, with plenty of space for display. The Rothschilds are remembered: their monogram is displayed in two rooms, there are portraits and caricatures of the family, and two old coaches from the Rothschild collection. The nucleus of the archaeological collection is an exhibit of prehistoric remains formed by F. Sadler, a former Borough Surveyor of Acton. Round it has grown a collection of maps, engravings and prints representative of the area in the past. Industrial archaeology has not been forgotten: there is a Stanhope printing press used by the Chiswick Press for some 40 years in the production of their fine books. There is an amateur painting of a Nevill's van, delivering bread from the 'patent steam ovens' in Acton. This is an unpretentious museum, well directed, with none of that tendency to an *omnium gatherum* evident in many small museums. The local collections are growing, and an attractively printed pamphlet history of the house and park has been published.

Pope's Lane, outside the park, is within the borough of Ealing: it is supposed to have been a favourite walk of Alexander Pope on his visits to the Earl of Warwick—but he must have been a tremendous walker if he came from Twickenham. Near here lived Dr. William Dodd, celebrated schoolmaster, author of *The Beauties of Shakespeare*—the last man in England to be executed for forgery. Another celebrated character, Charles Blondin the tightrope walker, lived here; there is no plaque, but Niagara House, a block of flats in Northfield Avenue, may remind the passer by of one of his exploits.

This district is, in fact, the centre of Georgian and Victorian Ealing, a place of winding streets, a few groups of cottages, gathered round the parish church of St. Mary, a massive piece of Victoriana with an enormous tower. Pevsner called it 'elephantine', Robbins writes: 'its elaborate ugliness defies description'; Nairn describes it as 'one of the most bewildering buildings in London'. The former Georgian church was a neat little building; the present St. Mary's was rebuilt by S. S. Teulon, from 1866-1873, and it was then hailed as 'basilican in appearance'. Having read all this, I was naturally anxious to see the inside, but every entrance was locked. The only piece of information on the front porch was a notice advising the public that there was no danger of fire, as one of the turrets was in use as a chimney for the heating system. Eventually the keys were found in the churchwardens' cottage in St. Mary's Place. The interior proved to be as ruthlessly grandiose as the exterior. Practically all the old monuments have been crowded into one end of the church. The only real antiquities are a fine brass to Richard Amundesham, Stapler of Calais, of the late fifteenth century. There is an alabaster tablet to Richard Taverner, vicar in 1638—with emblems of mortality: an hourglass, skull and cross bones. But other eighteenth-century tablets are a reminder of Ealing worthies, and some curious connections with the Johnsonian circle. There is John Horne Tooke, the radical who defended Wilkes, and renounced the cloth. He criticised Johnson in his philological works, and Johnson (for once) admitted that the criticism was valid. There is a tablet to Robert Orme, historian of the East India Company, the friend of Boswell. Finally there is the tomb of Sarah Trimmer, who astonished Johnson by producing a copy of

Milton from her pocket, in order to settle an argument about *Paradise Lost*. Mrs. Trimmer was a prolific writer of tracts, abridged the Old and New Testaments (they were best-sellers), worked for Sunday schools with Sturgess, one of the local vicars, and came here from the village of Brentford.

Round the church in the eighteenth and nineteenth century clustered Ealing's best schools, the largest of them (and the largest private school in England) being Ealing Great School. Nicholas, its headmaster, was famous, and the list of its scholars reads like a roll of honour. Thackeray and Marryat were there, Cardinal Newman and his brother, together with such Empire-makers as Sir Henry Rawlinson, Sir George Lawrence and Sir Henry Lawrence (all of whom distinguished themselves in India and Afghanistan); and later came William Hicks (Hicks Pasha). Thomas Henry Huxley was born in a house near the school, where his father was mathematics master; while Louis-Philippe of France was assistant master for a time. Dr. Dodd had a school at the old Manor House. Ealing House, another school, had one well-known scholar, Edward Bulwer Lytton. Anyone who has the perseverance to plough through the insufferably tedious *My Novel* can recognise scenes from Ealing and Norwood used as a background to a complicated plot : while 'Baron Levy' and his mansion are probably to be identified with Gunnersbury.

Coming from Little Ealing, there is a pleasant series of Victorian terraces, with many trees, and two parks, away from the traffic of the High Street. Lammas Park, formed from an old Common, is a pleasant little place : the larger is Walpole Park. Its chief feature is a remarkable house, Pitshanger Manor, now the Public Library. The south wing was built by George Dance the Younger in 1770, the centre portion by Sir John Soane in 1802, for his own residence. For a country villa (and this was little more) the frontage is grandiloquent, with four Ionic columns on which stand terra-cotta statues; a second floor, windowless, with carved panels; and, above this, a balustrade. There is an imposing entrance which leads into a small hall. Dance's wing is much more delicate : I saw it at its worst, for it was being redecorated after a fire. The dining-room and the drawing room upstairs are of noble proportions, with delicate stucco decorations. The hall is narrow, the staircase steep but with elegant balusters. The two largest rooms are used as Reading Room and Reference Library, the former containing a bronze plaque to T. H. Huxley. The modern lending library that has been added in 1940 to the older portions is lumpish and incongruous. Pitshanger was the old manor house, owned by a Quaker family before Soane redesigned it. Later tenants were the daughter of Spencer Percival, the Prime Minister who was murdered in the House of Commons in 1812, and Spencer Walpole, the Victorian Home Secretary.

The park itself is a fine place, famous for its trees, for each Mayor of Ealing has planted a tree in one fine avenue; there are, too, some remarkable cedars. There have been rumours of a four-lane highway which might thrust through the centre of the borough, affecting the park, the library and nearby Mattock Lane. In this lane is the Questors Theatre, possibly the finest amateur theatre in London. Certainly the centre of Ealing is overburdened with traffic, but so is every other 'Broadway' in London. To see what the motor car can do to a once quiet place, one should visit Haven Green, a small open space near the station. Now the Green is a large parking place for cars; half Ealing's bus services stop there; there is a periodic roar from the Central Station, where there are three stations in one. Superadded to this din, is the noise of planes coming into Heathrow Airport, three miles away. In spite of all this, old people doze on benches in the sun, children play on the grass.

Within a half mile of here is Ealing Green, where history of a different kind was made: the history of the British cinema. In a turning off the Green are the Ealing Studios, for 25 years the most productive unit in the country. From 1931, when the studios opened, until the 'forties not much emerged except a stream of indifferent dramas, thrillers and slapstick comedies. But during the Second World War there was a stiffening of fibre and a sense of purpose in a number of war films made by the young directors Charles Friend, Basil Dearden and Charles Crichton. Presiding over them was Michael Balcon providing finance (mainly on overdrafts), arranging distribution—but giving directors and scriptwriters a free hand. Most of these films were produced on a shoestring; many failed at the box office: but all were well scripted and cast with a set of young actors who were to become famous. It was in 1945, with Hamer's *It Always Rains on Sunday* that the Ealing realistic style emerged. *Hue and Cry* and *Passport to Pimlico* were the first Ealing comedies, precursors of a series that was to last for ten years. Outstanding productions, full of amusing situations, they projected the 'British way of life'. They were full of thoroughly British characters, every day, hard-headed, crusty or eccentric: the outstanding actors were given realistic lines by a brilliant series of script-writers headed by T. E. B. Clarke. Stanley Holloway, Basil Radford, Cecil Parker, Jack Warner, Joan Green-wood, Margaret Rutherford were only a few of the actors: and the protean Alec Guinness played the bank clerk in *The Lavender Hill Mob*, the shy young scientist in *The Man in the White Suit*, and eight characters in *Kind Hearts and Coronets*. The Ealing comedies came to an end in 1956 with *The Lady Killers*: tastes were changing, but British cinema has never been as good since. The comedies were never regarded as art: they were merely funny. 'Lacking money, Ealing made do with talent' was one comment. The studios were taken over by the British Broadcasting Corporation in 1957 for tele-vision production. Inside the entrance is a bronze plaque inscribed: 'Here many films were made projecting Britain and the British character'. This is, surely, part of Ealing's history.

Sir Michael Balcon, however, cannot be counted as one of Ealing's worthies. But in the square mile or so around the centre many well-known people have lived; although their houses may have gone, they may be traced in the local archives in the library. Among them were the Duke of Kent and Mrs. Fitzherbert; Henry Fielding the novelist lived near the Common, just before his last journey to Lisbon in 1754; the great publisher Archibald Constable lived near Castlebar Hill; Lady Byron was at Fordhook House, and her daughter Ada was married there.

From here the closest of Ealing's old villages is Hanwell, reached by going along Northfield Avenue. Hanwell Broadway is unpre-possessing, with two great bus depots, two gloomy looking ceme-teries, and narrow streets on either side. Its continuation is dominated by a vast Victorian Gothic complex of buildings, St. Bernard's Hospital, formerly the Hanwell Asylum for the insane poor. This was the West London counterpart of the North London Colney Hatch. Its most famous and enlightened governor was John Conolly, a pioneer of humane methods, who wrote: 'the great and only real substitute for restraint is invariable kindness'. Caroline Fox, after a visit to the asylum in 1842, wrote: 'it is a most delightful and heart cheering spectacle to see madness for once not treated as a crime'. Conolly, a true Victorian worthy, is commemorated in a tiny park near here: Conolly Dell.

Ealing's churches and chapels seem innumerable to the visitor: to be exact, however, there are 97 of them: 29 Church of England, 13 Catholic, and 54 of 'other denominations'. The Victorian churches are mostly uncompromising in stock brick, vast or inhospitable; while the majority of the modern churches are timid essays in pseudo-Gothic. Only the Catholics seem enterprising in their choice of architects and bold in their use of materials or decoration. There is one fine Catholic church (the Church of the Ascension) in the Hanger Hill area; and two modern churches in Hanwell are worth more than a cursory inspection. Edward Maufe's St. Thomas the Apostle has a splendidly austere interior, with a creative use of reinforced concrete to form a slender pointed vaulting; and here also is a masterly Crucifixion by Eric Gill. St. Mellitus, at the corner of Church Road, bulks large, with an elaborate sculptured entablature over the porch; inside is some fine modern glass by Christopher Webb.

Church Road leads into the old Hanwell Village, and to the parish church. St. Mary's is not in Giles Gilbert Scott's best style—Pevsner writes of its 'prim rectangularity'. The interior apparently contains only one monument of interest; the church (like so many today) is kept locked. There is, however, one reward to be found in the graveyard—the tomb of Jonas Hanway, philanthropist, founder of the Marine Society, famous for his work with the poor, and for Sunday Schools. He was a great pamphleteer, and his publication against tea-drinking inevitably raised Johnson's ire. He was an original, being the first man to use an umbrella in the streets of London, and persisting in the habit for 30 years until the umbrella was generally adopted. When he felt his powers failing, he paid his tradesmen, settled his affairs, and prepared for death. He also directed that he was to be buried here, for he was a frequent visitor to Hanwell, and a friend of the local vicar. 'As honest, energetic hard-working and true-hearted a man as ever lived', wrote Samuel Smiles who was a good judge of such men. So here he lies in Hanwell Village.

It is a true Victorian village, with neat houses and a green surrounded by fine trees. In the distance are the six great arches of Brunel's Wharncliffe Viaduct, a masterpiece of Victorian engineering. There are six cottages, all elegant; but one, The Hermitage, with its white walls, thatched roof, circular windows and ogival doorway a delight to look on. The village is quiet, for it is a dead-end and motors do not penetrate. A country lane leads into a pleasant park. Beyond is open space and a golf course, with the River Brent winding through it : no longer 'choked with water lilies', as one historian has it, the Brent is more like a country stream here than at any point in its upper reaches. Hanwell and its companion village have little visible that is historic; but prehistory is evident in Elthorne Park, where a great glacial boulder seems to indicate the final point of the Ice Age in Middlesex. A charter of Saxon times shows that land in the parish of Hanwell was owned by one Aelfwine, who, wishing to go on a pilgrimage to Rome, mortgaged it to St. Dunstan for '30 lb of silver'. Aelfwine returning home was unable to discharge his debt, 'whereupon the holy St. Dunstan suffered him to use the land all his life'. Sir Montague Sharpe, the author of *Middlesex in British Roman and Saxon Times*, records many incidents in Hanwell's history : he lived close to the village in Brent Lodge Park.

It might be interesting to follow the windings of the Brent to Perivale, another of the old Ealing villages, but there is no towpath, and no boats on the river. Ruislip Road leads to Western Avenue; on the one side is Perivale Park with the Brent winding through it, on the other a modern housing estate : the old village has virtually disappeared. Just off Western Avenue, the landmark being the tower of the Hoover factory, is Perivale Church, surrounded by trees. It is a picturesque place, with a small weatherboarded tower, and is reputedly the smallest church in Middlesex. The authorities give the date as thirteenth century: I noticed however that the board outside bore the earlier date of 1135. The interior was, I thought, as picturesque as the exterior, and had undergone a recent and most discreet restoration. The nave is only 50 feet long; there is a fine oak-beamed roof, and the monuments have been well-preserved. There is one very small brass of the sixteenth century to Henry Millet, his two wives, and (nicely grouped) their 16 children. Colourful fragments of mediaeval stained glass, found during the restoration, are embedded in the plain glass of the windows. There is a fine monument by Sir Richard Westmacott to Ellen Nicholas, daughter of the headmaster of Ealing Great School. Simon Coston, of a local family, gave the cover to the font in 1665. There is also a record of a contemporary donor—a photograph of Mr. Hoover, presenting a handsome cheque in aid of the restoration to the Rector. Going out of the church, I met the Rector himself. I asked him about the fifteenth-century Rectory. He explained that it had fallen down in 1958, there being no money to restore it; a new church and a new rectory had been built on the housing estate. Questioned about the date of the church, he told me that the experts who had assisted in the restoration had certified that a certain type of daub and wattle construction found there was undoubtedly of the reign of King Stephen. I congratulated him on the splendid restoration of the church; he then told me that much of it had been done under his own supervision, for he had once been a consulting engineer. Though most of the population have now moved to the newer part of Perivale, many still attend the services held here. I was doubly lucky in this encounter, for the Rector was there to lock up the church as a protection against vandals. This part of Perivale, with the Brent, the park and the golf course, is a pleasant place; although no longer the farmland which according to Michael Drayton grew 'the finest wheat in all England', it still preserves a semi-rural air.

The same atmosphere can be found in parts of Greenford, across Western Avenue, where Horsenden Lane runs up to Ealing's border with Harrow. Here are open spaces over a mile wide, with fields, woods, recreation grounds and a golf course. The Grand Union

Canal, deserted of traffic, runs under the lane; there are few houses except near the Ealing boundary; and Horsenden Wood is still a bird sanctuary of the Selbourne Society. The recreation ground has not been 'improved': the grass is rough, there are a few paths, a parking place and a belvedere. The hill is some 270 feet high, but the views are extensive: a useful bronze plaque indicates what to look for. Reading is marked (rather optimistically), but Windsor Castle may be glimpsed across the Middlesex plain. In one direction may be seen the Sydenham and the Surrey Hills; in another the Cities of Westminster and London; on the other side Highgate, Mill Hill and Harrow. In fact the greater part of Middlesex may be seen, in all its urbanisation, and with the remainder of its green fields. Horsenden Hill is a pleasant place in which to linger on a clear day; and although there might be a few more benches to sit on, one can only praise the enterprise which keeps this place clear and free of municipal asphalt. Horsenden, one chronicler of Greenford Parva writes, was a Celtic stronghold—'there are traces of this hill having been rudely fortified at a very remote period'. Montague Sharpe states that the Saxon standard of the White Horse (*Horsa-dun*) must have floated here. A good deal can be contrived, however, with the manipulation of the place names; the more prosaic 'Horsa's pasture' suggested by the authorities of the Place Name Society seems more likely. Whatever it was, Horsenden is one of the best viewpoints in Middlesex.

Finding what is left of Greenford is not as pleasant. Turning towards it from Western Avenue there is a huddle of factories, and the exotic street names of Uneeda Drive, Purex Avenue and Rockware Road. The village where Perkin had his chemical factory has disappeared under rows of red-brick houses, as has Greenford Green Farm, with its seventeenth-century barn. In the centre of the streets, which run into each other in a bewildering way, are two churches side by side in Ferrymead Gardens. They are both the Church of the Holy Cross, one seventeenth century, the other twentieth by A. E. Richardson. The twentieth-century church is one of Ealing's (and London's) finest, grand in exterior, austere inside with its timber vaulting. It is in the old church, with its typical weatherboarded tower, that traces of Greenford's history and its worthies may be found. The interior is fifteenth century with a lofty kingposted roof similar to that of Perivale; there is a small gallery and a primitive-looking organ. But the chief interest of the church is in its stained glass and its monuments. There are five great marble floor slabs, and some brasses including one to the Coston family, with father, his wife Bridget, a baby boy and five daughters. They gave the font here, as they did at Perivale. There is an interesting and well-crafted modern brass of 1917, to a rector with the curious name of Ogle Skan. The glass is fine, though fragmentary; on it appear the arms of Henry VIII and Katherine of Aragon, and of King's College Cambridge, which held the Rectory in the eighteenth century. Finally there is a tiny windmill, and two colourful lute-players. The glass is said to have come from King's College, though nobody can tell why or when. There are two mediaeval bells in the tower of this little church; and curiously, the modern church is kept locked, the old one, open.

The last of Ealing's villages, Northolt, is off Western Avenue on the border with Harrow and Hillingdon. It is a mixed neighbourhood, neither town nor countryside; factories along the arterial road, new roads overcoming the green fields, and much land awaiting development. The most conspicuous pointer to Northolt is the tall tower of the Aladdin factory: up Church Road a tiny village retains some of its personality. There is an inn, a few houses, a village green, a brook and three shops, including 'Ye olde Northolt Village store'. Behind on a green knoll is a small church, whitewashed with two heavy brick buttresses. It is generally kept closed as a protection against vandalism, but the keys, I found, were obtainable from a house on the nearby estate. St. Mary's has an austere interior of the fourteenth century, with only a few conspicuous monuments. There is a small gallery supported by Tuscan pillars, a fourteenth-century font, and one curiosity, a much embrowned painting of the Adoration, above the altar. There is one fine seventeenth-century brass of a vicar on the wall. The two best brasses are carefully protected by carpets. I had been told at the house that there had been much illicit rubbing of these brasses, another reason for keeping the church

closed. The chief curiosity, however, is a modern tablet to Gronow Owen, put here by the Honourable Society of Cymmorodion. The son of a tinker, educated at Jesus College, Oxford, he was curate of St. Mary's from 1755-57. But he was a Welsh poet also—'Master poet and prose writer in whose works the ancient dignity and beauty of the Welsh language shone forth anew'. He left Northolt abruptly —he was a drunkard—and finally emigrated to Virginia : an extraordinary person to find in a Middlesex village.

Except for this village remnant, there is little else to see in Northolt. The old manor of Islip has disappeared, and a small park remains : other monuments still in the records of the Royal Commission cannot be found. Nearer the Harrow border, there is Northolt Park, flanked by roads named after English racecourses. On a hill is an R.A.F. radio station. And there is, of course, the Airport, by which Northolt's name is best known; the countryside around has been blighted for a square mile, rough grass and scrub taking the place of cultivated fields and trees. Round the perimeter of the airport, offices, factories and warehouses have grown : there is a vast array of beacons on either side of the runways which run alongside Western Avenue. Built for the Royal Flying Corps in the record time of six months in 1915, it has grown considerably since then. During the Second World War it was a base of Fighter Command and played a considerable part in the Battle of Britain. The base became a target for the Luftwaffe, and the attacks reached a climax on the afternoon of 29th September 1940, when over 200 high-explosive bombs fell in the Greenford area. A wing of the Polish Air Force was stationed here for three years, and a monument surmounted by a great stone eagle commemorates their dead. The airport has often been used for the departure of V.I.P.'s on official missions, and Winston Churchill left here to inspect the crossing of the Rhine. The Ministry of Civil Aviation used Northolt as an airport until 1954, when it became again the property of the Royal Air Force; the growth of the gigantic Heathrow has made a civil airport at Northolt unnecessary. Today Northolt is used for R.A.F. transport planes, though civil aircraft are occasionally given permission to land; everything is kept operational, but little seems to happen there, the vil-

18 *Syon House: the Ante Room*

lages around no longer being afflicted by low-flying planes. Northolt is the end of Ealing, and the beginning of the newest of London's boroughs—Hillingdon.

CHAPTER EIGHT

Hillingdon and the Western Boundaries

Hillingdon has been called 'a collection of towns separated by grass'. Before 1945 it did not exist as an entity; it consisted of one borough —Uxbridge—and three urban districts: Ruislip and Northwood, Hayes and Harlington, Yiewsley and West Drayton. Sixteen miles from north to south, bordered by Hertfordshire and Buckinghamshire, nearly 40% of Hillingdon is 'green-belt' country. Much of the north is still rural; the south is becoming built up and industrialised, with a growing number of factories and two airports within the boundaries.

Hillingdon is a conglomeration: but within it exist some of the last scraps of countryside lamented by John Betjeman:

> *Out into the outskirt's edges*
> *Where a few surviving hedges*
> *Keep alive our lost Elysium*
> *Rural Middlesex again*

and to see these outskirts, the better approach is by the north, through Harrow and the Rickmansworth Road, and into Northwood. Once there the countryside becomes visible. There is much housing on the right of the road, but to the left there are hedges and copses, a few farms, glimpses of the occasional barn or a stand of cows. Much effort has been made to preserve and to plan in Ruislip and Northwood. In 1914 the urban district had the first town-planning scheme in England. The results of that planning are evident, from the Northwood Hills with their two well-preserved woods to Eastcote with its carefully kept seventeenth- and eighteenth-century houses. There are 50 of these 'monuments' listed in the Royal Commission's inventory of 1937. A few have disappeared, but the majority remain.

The parish church of Northwood is outside the village on the Rickmansworth Road. Holy Trinity, a plain mid-Victorian structure of 1854, designed by S. S. Teulon with none of the grandiose manner of his church at Ealing, is almost humdrum architecturally; but it is interesting in its associations, for when it was built, Northwood was a hamlet, a few miles from the Grosvenor seat at Moor Park in Hertfordshire. It was a Grosvenor, the first Baron Ebury, who financed the building of Holy Trinity, and six tombs of the Eburys flank the path leading to the entrance porch. Another conspicuous tomb in the churchyard is that to Sir Robert Morier, Britain's greatest ambassador to Russia, the stone surmounted by a massive cross of Siberian jasper, the gift of the Czar. There are Eburys and Moriers inside the church, and there is a Burne-Jones window commemorating a Grosvenor. Two of the original stained-glass windows were probably designed by Teulon, for they bear his initials; two others were made by Powell's of Harrow, a few miles from here. Various enlargements and additions have been made during the church's comparatively short history, all of them in keeping with its Victorian simplicity. The beautifully carved clergy and choir stalls in the chancel, by Alan Hurst, were a subject of controversy when they were installed, one churchwarden refusing to sign the faculty for their execution, and threatening resignation. Today, mellow in golden wood, these carvings of musical instruments are as much a part of the fabric as the Burne-Jones window. Holy Trinity is a good example of how care and endowment by a prosperous congregation can keep a church in being. The small church school being rebuilt is uncompromisingly of this century, and yet looks well, with the Victorian church as its neighbour.

Near to the church is Duck's Hill Road, which with Bury Street and Joel Street bound the most open part of Northwood. Duck's Hill, with a seventeenth-century farm at its highest point, winds gently down between Copse Wood, Mad Bess Wood, and Park Wood, with two golf courses beyond them. The houses are well spaced, the old ones well preserved, the modern ones discreet; the Actor's Charitable Homes, extended from an old house, are an elegant example of how this can be done. There is a shooting range, embellished by two notable eighteenth-century bronze cannon taken from the ill-fated H.M.S. *Association*. Sir Cloudesley Shovell, who wrecked his flagship in the Scillies, was not a Northwood man; the Mayfair gunsmiths who own the range, however, have fired both cannon on Trafalgar Day. The Lido, farther down the hill, was once a compensating reservoir for a canal; it is now a boating and bathing resort. The mounds near the Lido are earthworks, with the remains of a motte-and-bailey castle. The amateur archaeologist may explore the precinct of the castle, which belonged in the eleventh century to one Ernulf de Hesdin. This in fact is one of the most ancient parts of Middlesex, with more earthworks and a moat near Manor Farm in the High Street.

The High Street is a village at one end, a modern shopping centre at the other. At the crossroads stands the old village pump: the *Swan* is said to date from 1500, the old post office is picturesque with twisted chimneys, and there are some nice almshouses. The fine group of cottages in front of the church should be seen from the rear, where their timberwork is apparent. The church of St. Martin, though much restored (by the ubiquitous Gilbert Scott) has much antiquity left. The tower is fifteenth century, the nave thirteenth. In the north and south arcades are the remains of two mediaeval wall-paintings, much faded; but St. Michael, the Virgin, and St. Lawrence may be distinguished on one of them. The fifteenth-century roof of Middlesex oak is a splendid one; there are two massive sixteenth-century chests; and an ornately carved bread cupboard, for the poor of the parish, is dated 1697. A cluster of monuments, tablets and floor slabs are to the Hawtrey family, 25 of whom are commemorated here. This is the junior branch of the family, who originally came from Chequers. The Ralph Hawtrey of 1638 was a trustee of the Peace and lord of the manor; but none of them seem to have made much mark on history except Mary Hawtrey. She married Sir John

Bankes of Corfe Castle, and in his absence defended it twice against the Roundheads in the Civil War; the inscription on the monument states that she had 'borne with a constancy and courage above her sex a noble proportion of the late calamities'.

Away from the church, and going back to the Lido, is Manor Farm, with three fine barns, a garden, a moat, and the river Pinn. The farm and its surroundings once held a Priory dependent on the Norman abbey of Bec. The manor then went to King's College, Cambridge, then to Ruislip, who have kept the place in good trim. All the barns are well preserved; the largest, by a stroke of inspiration on the part of the Middlesex County Council, became a branch library. One can scarcely imagine a more elegant setting for books, a tall room, light and airy, very spacious, with thousands of volumes around the walls or in alcoves. A specially good collection of books on art is to be found here.

Between Eastcote Road and the High Road is a well-planned housing estate, with plenty of street trees. The most notable modern buildings are the schools, in Middlesex County's best style, with the Lady Bankes School in Dawlish Drive the best of them. Some parts of Eastcote House, the home of the Hawtrey family, remain in the public park Eastcote Place, near Field End Road. It is a hilly little park with fine trees. At the top of the rise are some melancholy-looking boarded-up buildings, the stables, with good old timberwork. There is also a massive seventeenth-century dovecot, covered with creeper, and a nicely kept walled garden. Eastcote and Field End Road are full of secluded houses, well kept, in a tree-lined setting. There are a number of wood barns in good preservation, and the few modern houses in this area are in 'Georgian' style, and do not assault the eye. Not all of the 50 listed in the inventory are still standing, but enough remain to make Eastcote the best preserved section of eighteenth-century Middlesex. South Ruislip, the modern section, has not much to recommend it: the housing is conventional.

The fields opposite Ruislip airport are flat, desolate and scrubby, with narrow canal feeders and the Yeading Brook almost invisible to the passing motorist on Western Avenue. Up Long Lane is Ickenham, once a village, now a separate estate of 'desirable residences', secluded and quiet. The remnants of a village green remain at the Swakelys crossroads, its village pump conspicuously preserved. Opposite a gaudy petrol station is the modern substitute for a village centre—Community Place—with a neat-looking branch library, a clinic, and a small hall housing the scouts, guides and Toc H—all very well arranged. The worthies of past Ickenham are to be found in the parish church of St. Giles set back a little from the main road. It is a charming little church, whitewashed, with a small spire, and a bell turret with four bells, the earliest dating from 1510. Much of the church is fourteenth and fifteenth century, and the interior with its fine timber roof is a perfect example of a village church. On the walls are memorials and brasses to the Says and the Shoreditches, lords of the manor and wardens of the church. Here also are the Vyners, the Haringtons and the Clarkes, owners of the great house of Swakelys. An elegant Jacobean wooden font is said to have been recovered from the house where it was being used as 'a tea-caddy or work table'. The chief curiosity of the church is the small pillared and arched St. John's chapel of about 1650. This was used as a mortuary chapel by the Haringtons of Swakelys: it once contained 30 coffins dating from 1647 to 1802, the bodies being subsequently reburied in the churchyard. There are still chiselled slabs to the Haringtons embedded in the walls, with an inscription to Elizabeth Harington, daughter of Sir James 'enshrined in this piller' (*sic*). There is also a tablet to Sir Robert Vyner, who died in Rome and whose body was brought back here for burial. Other memorials are in the body of the church, but the most beautiful is that of a shrouded baby, life size, in a window recess of the chancel. He is Robert, son of Sir Robert Clayton; his mother, Dame Martha, died within a few hours of his birth. On going out of the church there is in a niche a crumbling bust of the Earl of Essex; its companions are to be found in Swakelys House.

The search for Swakelys can be difficult and prolonged. Its park is enclosed by the modern estate of detached houses all widely spaced and full of dead ends. It lies in fact down the Avenue, where a notice board well concealed by trees reads 'Swakelys Sports Club'. The setting is magnificent, in a vast space of lawn surrounded by trees, and the house looks magnificent too, brown brick with plaster dressings, huge windows, pediments and curved gables. Originally built by Sir Edmund Wright between 1629 to 1638, it was improved by Sir James Harington and eventually bought by Sir Robert Vyner in 1663. Since then its exterior has changed little: it is now in the care of the Ministry of Works, having been owned by the Foreign Office Sports Association and finally going to London Postal Region, who use it as a sports club.

The chief feature of the hall at Swakelys is a massive wood screen with pillars, painted to resemble marble. In its curved pediment are two busts, one of Fairfax, one of Charles I—the third, of Essex, is to be found in the church. These must have been put there by Harington, who sat on the trial of Charles I, and fled to the Continent after the Restoration. There is a magnificent fireplace in a side room, and the panelling is as fine here as in the hall and staircase. The staircase has mural paintings and a painted ceiling. Colourful, rather pompous, with frozen attitudes, the symbolic figures of the mural are yet appropriate in their setting; they are attributed to Robert Streater. Pevsner dismisses them as 'poor work', but Streater was much admired in his day, being compared to Rubens, and even Michelangelo. They evidently appealed to Sir Robert Vyner, who admired grandeur. There is an example of this in the great 'parlour' on the first floor, its remarkable plaster ceiling divided into panels, with cherubs' heads and classical decoration. I should like to have seen the room in its original condition—it is now divided by an ugly softboard partition to form a games room, the original furniture gone and replaced by a litter of card tables and steel chairs. This was the room much admired by Pepys when he visited Vyner in search of a loan: 'his long gallery very fine above stairs, and better or such furniture I never did see'. After dinner Pepys was entertained here, 'to my great delight', by songs from a Mrs. Worship. He finally made his way home by Harlington, Brentford, and a boat on the Thames. Sir Robert Vyner was the greatest banker of his time, and a man of enormous wealth, lending freely to the King. He was ruined by the dishonest closing of the Exchequer in 1672, and it took an act of Parliament for him to get his money back. He became Lord Mayor of

120

London in 1674, and was reproached for his 'familiar and facetious' conduct to Charles II, when he entertained the King at Guildhall. So here was his great gallery now given over to whist and darts: no one can be blamed for this—certainly not the London Postal Region, for the refurbishing of this great place would strain even the National Trust's resources. One must be content that the fabric is sound and the building preserved. It is, surely, the most notable Jacobean house in Middlesex.

It is by the Great West Road and the Bath Road that one approaches the remaining part of Hillingdon; and between the Bath Road and the Great West Road goes one unmistakable fact of life in Middlesex—Heathrow Airport. There was once a Heath Row village and a Heath Row House—both swallowed up by the expanding airport. A Romano-Celtic temple was discovered when the land was being excavated, with pottery finds of the Iron Age about 300 B.C., so Heathrow is among the most ancient and most modern places of Middlesex. There are seven square miles of Heathrow, 13 miles of perimeter roads; 47,000 people work there; round it have been gathered factories, storage depots and hotels; Heathrow is a town in itself. The repercussions of the existence of Heathrow— complaints about noise—extend over half London and the Home Counties. The problem of the noise in the immediate area is severe, if not insoluble, for there are acres of housing and many schools. The Wilson report on air noise recommended subsidies for double glazing in nearby housing estates. A school in Cranford has recorded 110 decibels of noise (the acceptable limit is 45); another school after spending £60,000 on double glazing has given up, and the site has been sold for yet another airport hotel.

Heathrow is worthy of examination, however, not by the passenger rushing to catch a flight, but by the sightseer. The perimeter roads are an industrial slum, lined with dozens of small buildings, store-rooms for airlines: only a few hotels mitigate the squalor. One of them, the Ariel, is a distinguished piece of architecture—a great cylinder of glass brick and mosaic, with an interior courtyard; inside the hotel is an extraordinary spiral staircase which floats upwards, and there is a hushed quiet. The long tunnel that leads to the three terminal buildings is an impressive piece of engineering; once out of it and circulating round a mazy series of roads, everything is on a large scale, the three terminal buildings, the multi-storey car parks and the hangars. Over them all looms Sir Owen Williams' control tower, bleakly grand. On entering Terminal Two and going up the escalators, one can sense the organisation behind the airport. The huge concourse on the first floor, in spite of hundreds of people moving about, is quiet; rather comforting, with none of the covert hostility of the new railway stations. On black leather benches people stare at the huge board announcing flights to every capital in Europe: the staff everywhere are polite, efficient and reassuring. Up half a flight of stairs is a spacious lounge and bar where one can get one of the best (and cheapest) cups of coffee in the London area, near it is a 'waving point'. There is plenty to do here if one has an hour or so to spare: organised trips round the control centres, watching the planes, even an excursion on a flight simulator. Upstairs, then, is fairly serene: it is only downstairs in the departure lounges that an atmosphere of suppressed hysteria can be felt. Beneath the main runway is an interdenominational chapel for the staff. There is, too, a garden which someone called 'the noisiest garden in the world'. Well beyond the runways and in the fields can be found (with some searching) a narrow ribbon of water, the Duke of Northumberland's river, and the Longford river: these rivers are feeders from the Colne river. Constructed in Charles I's time, for drinking water, they now supply the ornamental waters at Hampton Court.

Hayes and Harlington, formerly a borough, is nearest to Heathrow. There were once four villages here, Cranford, Yeading, Hayes and Harlington. Three have been almost submerged by housing and factories, and the district is cut into slices by arterial roads. Cranford, on the map, looks the most rewarding, for there is a large patch of green. The village is best approached from the Bath Road and Southall High Street. The approach from the north is full of blind turnings and blocked lanes, and the motorist is led, inexorably, to the M.4 motorway.

Cranford Park is spacious, some half mile long, very open but surrounded by trees; at one end lies the motorway, at the other a few streets of housing. Here the river Crane appears after rising 15 miles away in Pinner; afterwards it disappears under the Bath Road, eventually running into the Thames at Isleworth. It is a pleasant stream at Cranford, but there are no cranes (or herons) here now. In a small corner of the park are the village church and the remains of the once very grand Cranford House.

The difficulty of visiting a church on a Saturday afternoon is that people will get married. The bells of St. Dunstan's were ringing a peal when I went there, and the bride and groom were being photographed. But this was all part of the village atmosphere. Campanology is a rare enough thing in Middlesex; and the bells of St. Dunstan's, the earliest dating from 1380 have, they say, rung for every great victory from Agincourt to Alamein. The stables close by the church are the only remaining part of Cranford House, and only part of the stables is left. There are six large brick arches, with a two-storeyed building, the windows boarded up, the interior floors rotting. The building may be taken over as a design studio and rehabilitated without being spoiled. The big 200-year-old clock is still keeping good time, and a bronze plaque records the demolition of the great house in 1945. The stables were the headquarters of the Berkeley, which hunted over all this part of the Middlesex plain. Its leader was Grantly Berkeley, the most choleric sportsman of his time, who in his *Reminiscences of a Huntsman* records his exploits and the ghosts of Berkeley House. The last Berkeley left Cranford in 1918.

The wedding was over. Inside the church I found myself in a gathering of 12 people. They were all members of the Middlesex Society, on one of their weekly excursions. We exchanged impressions, laboriously deciphered inscriptions together; they were all amateur historians and eager to learn, and the copy of Pevsner's book I had brought with me was passed from hand to hand. There is much to see in Cranford church; it has been greatly restored but its monuments are kept with care. The finest of these is to Sir Roger Aston, King James's Keeper of the Wardrobe, and owner of Cranford House; here he kneels with his two wives opposite and his five daughters around him: the figures are contained in an elaborate setting of an arch with four Corinthian columns. There is one fine Berkeley tomb in the church—Lady Elizabeth, Ann Boleyn's cousin, who purchased the manor in 1618. Her figure seems to emerge from the marble slab, the face serene, the head covered by a flowing veil with a curious circular top-knot. The tomb is by Nicholas Stone: the church records that it was made in Bernini's studio in Rome. Here too are echoes of the Civil War, in a tablet to Thomas Fuller, Rector of Cranford from 1658-61: he was chaplain to Sir Ralph Hopton during the war, became Chaplain to Earl Berkeley, and accompanied him to the Hague in 1660 to meet Charles II. Author of *The Worthies of England*, he was much admired by Pepys, both for his learning, and for his memory: he could tell Pepys 'more of my own family than I knew myself'. There is a tablet to Sir Charles Scarburgh, physician to Charles II, one of the most learned men of his time, and one of the original Fellows of the Royal Society. He was a friend and colleague of Thomas Harvey who, in his will, left him 'all my little silver instruments of Surgerie'. Sir Charles himself, the tablet records, went from his life 'by no violent distemper, but a gentle and easy decay'—a meet epitaph for a great surgeon.

There is so much to see in this little church: a naïve painting on glass of St. Jerome with his lion; another painting of the Assumption from Cuzco in Peru; a brass commemorating the death of an old man killed by a wolf. There is also a 'Musical' stained glass window—does its quotation from *Elijah* confirm the legend that Mendelssohn played the organ here?

Cranford village is gradually disappearing. There are indeed a few fine Georgian houses left, notably Stansfield House. But where was the village pond, where The Cedars, where the great Isambard Kingdom Brunel lived? The Round House Observatory has been demolished, and there is nothing to mark the place where Warren de la Rue, 'eminent in celestial photography', worked: he was the most famous astronomer of Victorian times. Even the good habit of naming streets after local worthies is in abeyance—there is a Berkeley Avenue only. Not far from here on the Bath Road is a twentieth-century substitute for a parish church—the church of Holy Angels—

built of steel, and with, I was told, a hooter instead of a peal of bells. Perhaps this is appropriate, however, in a factory area, close to Heathrow Airport.

The remains of Harlington village are in a section of the High Street bounded by the Bath Road and the M.4 motorway. Turning into the High Street there is the William Byrd School, so named because the great Tudor composer lived here from 1577-1592, when he was in the Chapel Royal. Harlington is one of the oldest villages in Middlesex, known as far back as A.D. 831, when its name is given in the Saxon Cartularies as Hygereding Tun. The name has undergone a number of changes since then, even to Arlington when that title was taken by Sir Henry Bennet, on ascent to the peerage. He was the Arlington of the notorious Cabal government, and the tomb of his grandfather Sir John Bennet can be found in the parish church.

SS. Peter and Paul is one of the oldest Middlesex churches. It has a three-storey tower surmounted by a cupola, and the building is set in a well kept churchyard; there is the stump here of a great yew tree, said to be over a thousand years old and still giving out vigorous branches. The Norman doorway of the church is elaborately pillared and is carved with curious decoration which Pevsner describes as 'beakhead'; the description by the church authorities describes them simply as 'cats' heads'. The interior glows with colour from stained glass windows. There is much evidence of the age of the church—the first rector is described as '1086—The Priest of Herdinstone'; there is another rector, John Monemouth, commemorated on a brass of 1419. There are brasses of the fifteenth and sixteenth centuries, a twelfth-century font, an unusual 'Easter Sepulchre' of the fourteenth century, and much more of architectural interest. The most elaborate monument is to Sir John Bennet, lord of the Manor, with two of his three wives—three fine busts framed in an archway, with underneath them a tablet surrounded by garlands of flowers and three delightful cherubs. But the most interesting monuments are to the de Salis family, commemorated in the stained glass windows, and in the tablets on the walls; they were owners of one of the manors, Dawley Court. Here are generations of warriors, among them Louis de Salis of the Scots Guards, Leopold Fane de Salis, and mightiest of them all, Lieutenant General Rudolph de Salis, who as Colonel led the 8th Kings Irish Royal Hussars in the charge of the Light Brigade. Another stone monument over a doorway shows his commanding visage with all his battles in the Crimea and Indian Mutiny arrayed beside him. The de Salis family is one of the most notable in Middlesex: they are to be found not so much in the *Dictionary of National Biography* as in the *Almanach de Gotha*. The first of them, one Peter de Salis, came to England as an envoy in 1709. The men of the family were many of them Swiss mercenary soldiers; and they have bred mostly soldiers since they emigrated to England in 1793, becoming British nationals. Their twentieth-century descendants include two lieutenant-colonels, two eminent divines, and Sir Cecil Fane de Salis, who was Chairman of the Middlesex County Council from 1920 to 1925. Appropriately enough the living line includes a de Salis who is a publisher of military histories. Dawley Court was demolished in the 'twenties, only an elaborate gateway to a housing estate in Corwell Lane marking the spot.

So much for the details revealed by a village church. There is little else in brick or stone to remind one of Harlington's past: the place was, up to early in this century, agricultural land, famous for its cherry orchards—there is a reminder of the fact in Morello Avenue, Cherry Gardens and Whitehart Avenue. There is not much open space save for a few playing fields. Harlington and Hayes, once two separate villages, have now merged into one township. The Yeading area on the Ealing border has little to commend it: the Yeading Brook, almost concealed by hundreds of houses, shops and flats, with many factories, meanders through this area.

Hayes itself has become much industrialised, though there is still some semblance of green in its centre round Church Walk, with the Town Hall (now one of the widely scattered offices of the Borough of Hillingdon), the church, and another Manor House, where Cranmer is alleged to have lived for some time. The church of St. Mary, much of it belonging to the thirteenth to fifteenth centuries, is interesting, though much 'altered and improved' by Giles Gilbert Scott. It has interesting memorials to the Fenner family and a mediaeval wall painting of St. Christopher. But Hayes is, on the whole, a spoilt village, in spite of a few good old houses. Dawley Manor, bought by Henry St. John Viscount Bolingbroke from the Bennet family, has now been demolished. Here Bolingbroke, after a long and turbulent political career, settled as a sort of hermit-philosopher in a mansion 'politely furnished, elegantly grand, frugal of ornament but that the best'—which he preferred to call a farm. Here he lived and philosophised, entertaining such friends as Dryden, Voltaire and Alexander Pope—who embodied some of Bolingbroke's *dicta* in his *Essay on Man*. There are many accounts of Dawley, where the hospitality included lighting Bolingbroke's guests on the road to West Drayton by 'artificial lanterns'. But where the mansion actually was is a matter of conjecture. Robbins (who is generally right) says it was demolished in 1744. The Borough's guide states that it was preserved, until 1951, within the precincts of the great factory of Electrical and Musical Industries, known throughout the world as His Master's Voice. It is a great sprawling place, dominating this part of Hayes and visible from both arterial roads. The firm shows parties round the works at weekends, and one can see the routine miracle of a blob of black plastic being pressed between two circular plates and turning into a Beethoven symphony.

The Middlesex border with Buckinghamshire contains more villages which are growing into suburbs. The land was up to the late nineteenth century mainly agricultural. Now slowly but surely it is becoming permeated by industry and the housing necessary to it. The nearer to the Bath Road, the more industry; the farther away the more countryside; in the centre is Uxbridge, a county township.

Yiewsley and West Drayton, formerly an urban district, used to call itself the Gateway to England, for Heathrow Airport lay within its boundaries. The southern part of the district is cut in half by the M.4 motorway, and then into more sections by a natural river, the Colne, and two artificial waterways, the Wyrardisbury and the Duke of Northumberland's River. In this part are preserved, to some extent, two villages, Sipson and Harmondsworth. Sipson dates from the thirteenth century, when it was 'Subwines Farm'—today it is a place without much character. Harmondsworth is older still, being first mentioned in 1086. Here are some remains of a village, with a few old buildings. Scarcely anyone knew of Harmondsworth, save antiquaries, until 1936, when Penguin Books established their headquarters there. Nowadays this Middlesex place name is known all over the world from the imprint on millions of title pages of paperbacks. Harmondsworth's chief attraction is its great medieval barn, the best preserved in Middlesex. It is 190 feet long, 36 feet wide, with 12 bays and an impressive tiled roof. There are traces of a moat near the barn, and the records show that a Benedictine Abbey of Rouen once stood here. The church of St. Mary in the village street has a good tower, with a cupola. The doorway is Norman, the interior varying from thirteenth to sixteenth century: some of the pews are from the latter period. But it has few memorials of interest, and all the brasses are said to have been stolen in the middle of last century—so church vandalism is no recent phenomenon. Some pleasant old buildings remain in the High Street and help to preserve something of a village atmosphere. The widening of the Bath Road seems to have put an end to the idea of extending the Airport northward, as prophesied by one of the Middlesex historians. But further factory building in Harmondsworth seems as inevitable as its encroachment into West Drayton.

At first glance West Drayton seems to be an agglomeration of houses and factories, with little sign of planning. Certainly little of its horticulture and market gardening seems to have survived save for a firm in Money Lane, famous throughout Europe for their splendid pansies and anemones. The factories are for gear wheels, screws, nuts, coachbuilding, civil engineering. The factories of Middlesex vary much in size and appearance. Some of them are monumental, like Gillette, Peerless or Hoover; many of the middle-sized ones can be neat and attractive; far too many are grey, hastily built and badly cared for, with the inevitable piles of scrap in their yards. There are a few exceptions: one of them is a minor masterpiece—the Technicolor factory on the Bath Road: discreet, well detailed, with an apt use of colour.

A diligent quartering of the streets of West Drayton is, however, rewarding: there are still some vestiges of the old village, and from

19   Osterley House

20   Osterley House : The Orangery

them can be gathered facts about the people who lived here. The council offices on Sipson Road are themselves deceptive, looking like a handsome Victorian mansion. But this is Drayton Hall, previously the manor house of the Fysh de Burgh family, and here Napoleon III lived for a time.

The real pleasure of West Drayton is its extensive village green, with an avenue leading to the remains of the old Manor House and to the church. The green is a long rectangle surrounded by houses, some of them seventeenth and eighteenth century: conspicuous among them are the Old House and Southlands. There is indeed a rather drab row of Victorian cottages—Daisy Villas of 1896; but even these have a faded charm. The trees are fine, both in the green and around. Tucked in a corner at one end is Avenue Close and House, with a barn; leading out of the corner is the oddly named Courting Alley; at the other end of the green are two charming old shops with leaded panes. The village was remodelled by the Pagets when they built the Manor House in 1550 and the walls in the avenue leading up to it are obviously very old. Parts of the Manor House remain: in deep red brick, with battlements over a massive Tudor gateway. The side walls remaining form an enclosure to the church of St. Martin. Although heavily restored outside, the interior is, much of it, fifteenth century. The font is a fifteenth-century masterwork, octagonal, with carved figures—'the most elaborate in the county', writes Pevsner. The memorials begin with fifteenth-century brasses, continuing to Victorian times with a Burne-Jones window to a Mrs. Mercer. The finest memorial is to Rupert Billingsley, captain of the *Royal George*, which went down in 1782 with 800 men and Admiral Kempenfelt aboard, and is remembered in Cowper's poem:

> *A land breeze shook the shrouds*
> *And she was overset*
> *Down went the Royal George*
> *With all her crew complete.*

The tablet beneath Billingsley's epitaph has a fine carving of a three-

21 *Manor House, Southall*

masted vessel. There are three memorials to the De Burghs, second in succession as lords of the Manor, who lived at Drayton Hall. The Pagets who built the Manor are said to be buried upright beneath the raised aisle. They were indeed an extraordinary family. The first, Sir Willam, was an ambassador for Henry VIII, and comptroller of the household to Edward VI. Thomas, his son, was concerned in the Throgmorton conspiracy, fled to France, and his estates were seized. William, fifth in line, was restored to his estates; he too was an individualist, changing from Parliamentarian to Royalist at the outbreak of the Civil War; his estates were also sequestered. The seventh Lord Paget became Earl of Uxbridge, and it was an Earl of Uxbridge who succeeded Bolingbroke as owner of Dawley Court.

One could spend a long time tracing those memorialised in West Drayton church. Who for instance was Joseph Tiercelin of Nanteuil, 'most respected inhabitant of Piccadilly', who died here aged 92? And how came he to West Drayton with his family? He is not commemorated in any other way in this area, as are the de Burghs, by a fine hotel in Yiewsley, which still retains a seventeenth-century air about it. Yiewsley is very much of this century. On the main road going to Cowley, however, is another neat little inn called the *Paddington Packet Boat*: this is a reminder of the pleasure boat that plied on the canal from Uxbridge to Paddington until about 1850. Down Packet Boat Lane to the Grand Union Canal one still finds some activity on the waterway. Cowley, once a separate village, is now indistinguishable from Hillingdon. In St. Lawrence it possesses a tiny church of the twelfth century which vies with Perivale as being the smallest in Middlesex. And somewhere in the churchyard Dr. Dodd (of Ealing), executed for forgery, is buried: presumably only because his brother was rector.

Hillingdon, from which the whole of the area takes its name, is a prosperous district full of good housing and with plenty of street trees. With Uxbridge, this may be the centre of the new borough. Brunel University has moved here: the handsome new buildings are placed in a parkland of 175 acres, and there are now 2,000 students and staff. Hillingdon is a likeable place, with no lack of open space. It has led a separate existence for centuries. It appears in

Domesday Book as Hildendum, and its two manors included Icken-ham and Cowley. It possesses a fine parish church in St. John the Baptist, and within it is yet another Paget memorial—Henry, First Earl of Uxbridge. Hillingdon House, built in 1717, is referred to in Greville's Diary. Cox, the great banker, lived here in 1842, and the diarist, contrary to his general habit, had nothing but good to say of it: 'I never go to that place without looking with envy and admiration at a scene of so much happiness'. A less happy visitor to Hillingdon was Charles 1, who stopped at the *Red Lion* after his flight from Oxford.

Coming from Hillingdon Hill into Uxbridge, the most conspicuous object is the impressive entrance to the large R.A.F. Depot—a his-toric place, for this was Fighter Command Headquarters during the Battle of Britain. Uxbridge is a place which seems not yet to have decided whether to be a typical market town, or a twentieth-cen-tury minor metropolis. There are many aspects of the market town in the winding High Street, with its half-timbered or Georgian houses, and its remarkable pillared Market House. But the London Transport station is too obviously commanding. Near it appears a vast white concrete complex of buildings: the new town centre, including flats, shops, two supermarkets and 100,000 square feet of offices. Pedestrian walkways are on two floors and eventually the High Street will be closed to motor traffic. The parish church of St. Margaret is wedged into a narrow street off the main road. Inside its architectural interests include a splendid hammerbeam roof; outside, its flint-dressed walls and stone entrance are grime-blackened. There are still some fine old houses in Windsor Street, and two very plain but impressive buildings, the old Congregational Church and the Friends Meeting House. Going out of town, towards Denham, there is one historic building, *The Crown*. This was once the house of Sir John Bennet and one of its wings is the 'Treaty House' where the Commissioners met in 1645 to discuss the ending of the Civil War. But even here a wing was demolished for road widen-ing, and the interior panelling was shipped off to the United States in 1929. The remains of *The Crown*, however, look well kept and elegant and the brewers have lost no opportunity of reminding the passer-by of its historic associations. Down the hill behind the High Street lies the Canal and the river Colne, with some of the flour mills on which the township's prosperity was originally founded: many of the millers were of the Society of Friends, and there is a history of Quakerism and Dissent in this area. George Fox records the burning of three martyrs at the stake in 1555—the inhabitants say this was in Lynch Green, now Windsor Street. Uxbridge, then, has a long and at times turbulent history, including riots in 1630 against tolls taken by the Lady of the Manor, Alice, Countess of Derby, who lived in Harefield.

There were at one time 25 farms in Harefield; some, such as Cripps Farm and Colney Farm, may be traced back to the early fourteenth century. The district is rich in old buildings, and the search for them can be absorbing, though at times frustrating. Harefield Place, once an old manor house, is now a hospital. In Moorhall Lane there was at one time Moor Hall, a chapel of the thirteenth century belonging to the Hospitallers of St. John. I found at the end of the lane by the canal a miniature marina, with boats of all sizes, lying in a basin formed by old gravel pits. Here at any rate the Grand Union Canal has some boating activity—and there is more on the River Colne beyond it. But Moor Hall had, I was told, 'fallen down', and the cottages marked on the map had disappeared.

The High Street of Harefield is pleasantly varied, with a motley of houses of all periods, the twentieth-century ones discreet with dark wood boarding, the old houses mellow in red brick. The shops are village shops, though a nationally known bank has put up an obtrusive fascia board in black and gold: but this is essentially a village street, with three inns, one of them half timbered, the *King's Arms*, at the end of the village green. Farther on the road becomes a deep lane, with at its side the picturesque Cripps Farm and cottages. Then there is a no-man's land with a quarry, and at the foot of the hill a glimpse of Buckinghamshire, with the works of the Colne Valley Water Company and two reservoirs, Springwell Lake and Stocker's Lake. Running alongside them is the ribbon of the Grand Union Canal. This then is the remotest corner of Middlesex.

Another country lane alongside the village green passes the

ancient Colney Farm and leads to Breakspear, the manor of the Ashbys. Going down a drive, the first building visible is a massive square seventeenth-century dovecot, in deep red brick, with a cupola. The manor lies to the side overlooking a valley: it too is seventeenth century, with a few later additions. The leaded glass windows have stained glass coats of arms inserted: the entrance hall is finely panelled. Breakspear, after coming into the possession of the Tarleton family, has now become an old people's home. There are traces of the Tarletons in the copse behind the house; one of them had planted a great chestnut tree, another had turned the first sod of the carriage drive. Everything in the garden is settled, mellow and peaceful. Suddenly one noticed that it was quiet: there were wagtails on the lawn, and a pheasant suddenly appeared in the copse. Breakspear is indeed a fine and private place. The family were here in 1371 and not far away in Ruislip, a century earlier, legend connects them with the line that produced Nicholas Breakspeare, who became Adrian IV, the English pope. But he was no man of Middlesex.

The Countess of Derby's almshouses belong to the early seventeenth century. They are picturesque, in a curious H-shaped formation, brick with stone facings. The church, St. Mary the Virgin, is in a fold of the valley with a spacious graveyard round it; irregularly shaped with a small tower, it is not very impressive externally. But the interior, mainly of the fourteenth century, is a revelation, so crowded is it with monuments, memorial tablets, brasses, hatchments and church furniture. Here are the Ashbys, the Newdigates (who held manors in Harefield from the fourteenth to the twentieth centuries), the Tarletons, and a solitary Breakspeare, who married George Assheby and died in 1474. There is an elaborate memorial to John Pritchett, former curate of Harefield, afterwards Bishop of Gloucester. He was evicted from the city church of St. Andrew Undershaft during the Civil War, but was afterwards 'restored and elevated' by Charles II.

The total effect of the church's interior is overwhelming. The elaborate altar rails and the carving round the translucent glass commandment boards are Flemish, of the seventeenth century. The tombs of Lady Mary Newdigate and Sarah Newdigate are by Grinling Gibbons. Other monumental sculptures are by John Bacon, junior, Sir William Taylor, and Rysbrack. Three monumental urns, for his mother and his two wives, were erected by Sir Roger Newdigate, founder of the Newdigate Prize at Oxford. The epitaphs (some of them orations) would require a separate study. Mary Juliana Newdigate must have been a lady of some charm—'her good sense, polite behaviour and agreeable conversation were confessed by all that had the happiness of her acquaintance'. By the altar, lies the greatest Lady of Harefield.

Alice Spencer, Countess of Derby reclines in a splendid Jacobean tomb, her three daughters in niches beneath her. After her second marriage to Sir Thomas Egerton, Lord Chancellor, she became the Lady of Harefield Manor. In her youth, Edmund Spenser dedicated his *Tears of the Muses* to her; she was the 'Sweet Amaryillis' of his *Colin Clout's come home again*; John Marston wrote an entertainment for her; she played the part of Zenobia in Ben Jonson's *Masque of Queens*. In 1633, when she was 72, Milton wrote *Arcades* for her, and it was performed in the avenue of Harefield Manor 'by some noble persons of her family, who appear on the scene in pastoral habit, moving towards the seat of state'. Some historians state that Milton was present at the performance, for he was living at Horton, some 12 miles away: modern scholars say that Milton was not a personal acquaintance of the Countess. At any rate, Henry Lawes was here, for he composed the music for the masque and was music teacher to the Countess's grandchildren.

All this would be a fine scene to summon up in a *Son et Lumière* performance in the churchyard; and the Manor was very near the church. Elizabeth I came here for three days at the end of July 1602, in the course of her progress of Middlesex. There were great celebrations, and it must have been a very expensive visit for the Egertons: the account for one item alone, 'Players, Vaulters and Dancers', was £64. 18. 10d. The legend that Shakespeare and his players performed *Othello* is probably apocryphal—most authorities agree that the play was not written until 1604. It is not surprising that legends have grown about Harefield Manor, it was burnt down in 1660, some say it was by the carelessness of Sir Charles Sedley, who was remiss with his candles while reading in bed.

The burial ground outside Harefield church has much of interest. There are a number of old 'bed-post' tombstones, and the habit of memorialising the family servants on the church wall is unusual. There are four on the North wall, the most conspicuous being that of Robert Mossendrew, a faithful gamekeeper—portrayed walking through the fields with his gun and his spaniel, a flight of birds in the sky, and 14 lines of laudatory verse. The most conspicuous tombs in the burial ground are 110 in number, all uniform, to the Australian soldiers who died in Harefield Hospital during the 1914-18 War. The tombs are interspersed with rosebeds and an austere archway leads to them. An obelisk records that Sir Francis Newdigate, Governor of Western Australia, was instrumental, with the owner of Harefield Place, in arranging the memorial here.

Thus past and present link in Harefield church, and in the village which is an epitome of rural Middlesex. Long may it remain so.

CHAPTER NINE

Chiswick, Brentford and Isleworth

April 1965 was a date of significance for Middlesex. Many of its boroughs were then amalgamated into what were called 'viable units'. One of the most interesting of these amalgamations brought Hounslow into being. This was a case where the whole (comprising Brentford and Chiswick, Heston and Isleworth and Feltham) was named after one of its parts. Hounslow is extensive, with its eastern border in Hammersmith, its western border in Hillingdon and Heathrow airport; north is Ealing, south the curve of the Thames and the County of Surrey. It is a diversified place which varies from the Augustan sophistication of Chiswick to the great factories and office blocks that form a fringe to the arterial roads of Osterley and Isleworth, with their attendant housing estates. Over 200,000 people live in its 14,600 acres, yet there is still room for the great parks of Syon and Osterley, and lesser ones in Chiswick and Brentford, all of them with historic houses.

The approach to Chiswick from Gunnersbury Avenue leads to one of the most complicated road systems in Middlesex, with a confusion of road signs and main roads leading in all directions. Above all this the flyover to the M.4 motorway towers some 50 feet. Beneath its elephantine arches crouch a few streets of once pleasant suburban homes. Beyond them the high rise office blocks and sleek factories start to multiply. Ian Nairn calls the flyover 'blundering and messy'. It is certainly inhuman in its scale.

Chiswick High Road, though no longer a village High Street, is smaller in scale, and less noisy. Most of its older houses have dis-

appeared, with blocks of flats replacing them. The tall I.B.M. building dominates one side of the road. On the opposite side is Empire
House, built on the site of the Chiswick Empire, one of the last
suburban music-halls. Half way along the road is a small grass patch
called Turnham Green, still used occasionally for cricket matches.
Here, too, is Chiswick's Victorian Town Hall, now looking rather
forlorn, reduced, as it is, to a single municipal department. In
Barley Mow Passage (named after its picturesque inn) there is one
conspicuous building : Voysey House, once a factory, now owned by
an Assurance Company. The building, with its white walls of glazed
brick, its dark buttresses, wavy parapets and elegant windows is a
delightful example of late-Victorian simplicity. Charles Annesley
Voysey was a domestic architect famous for his fine houses—'his
work', wrote John Betjeman, 'was perhaps the finest flowering of
actual self-conscious architecture in Victorian England'. It is pleasant
to find his only factory preserved in this way—typical of much of
Chiswick, where there is, undoubtedly, a sense of the past. The street
names here echo the names of former residents: Hogarth Lane;
Paxton, Cavendish and Chatsworth Roads; Devonshire Gardens; and
Burlington Lane, which leads down towards Chiswick House.

Openings in the old wall that runs along Burlington Lane give a
glimpse, for example, of the obelisk which terminates three avenues
leading to the 'artificial river' in Chiswick Park. The main entrance is
in Chertsey Road. Once inside the park the scale of the place may be
seen: intimate rather than grand, with the house a Palladian-style
villa set at the end of an avenue lined with classic busts on pedestals.
The most striking feature is the main floor, with its six Corinthian
columns, entablature and a flat dome above; and a double staircase
leading up to it—the classic Italian *piano nobile*. The entrance to
the house is below, a dark tunnel-like opening set in grey rusticated
masonry. This is the villa created by Richard Boyle, third Earl of
Burlington, between 1720 and 1726. It was not a house, but a temple
of the arts, to display his collections and his library : above all it was
a place for meetings of his friends, the artists, and architects, poets
and philosophers of his time. There was a residence in the park, a
Jacobean house where, writes John Charlton in his guide, 'the

ordinary affairs of life, like sleeping and eating, were to continue.'

Chiswick Villa has been restored, after 20 years of neglect, by the Ministry of Works and is now unique and remarkable. The ground floor contains a curious series of rooms within rooms, all doorless, like a set of Chinese boxes. They housed Burlington's library, and now exhibit prints of the architectural designs of Colen Campbell, whose ideas doubtless inspired Burlington in his design of the villa. Beneath them is a neat little circular wine cellar, just big enough to house the 50 dozen bottles necessary to lubricate Burlington's symposiums. The main floor is reached by an inconspicuous spiral staircase, and here the real splendour of the villa is evident. The rooms, with great plaster ceilings designed by William Kent, are embellished with baroque fireplaces and classical statuary, and culminate in the remarkable 'domed saloon' now hung with a fine collection of pictures, brought back here from Chatsworth House. The 'red velvet' and 'blue velvet' rooms have some luxury, but the total effect is cold, calculated, philosophical; perhaps as Burlington intended. The Ministry of Works, in their restoration have done remarkably well. But they might have been a little less purist—a few discreet direction signs would do no harm; and there is nowhere to sit down except in the domed saloon.

Chiswick House has a long and interesting history. Its second owner was the fourth Duke of Devonshire; he demolished the old Jacobean house, and enlarged the villa with two wings designed by James Wyatt. And here for many years the Dukes of Devonshire entertained the great men and women of their time. Here Georgiana Duchess of Devonshire, 'reigning queen of eighteenth century society', held court. The house was the summer residence of Edward VII when he was Prince of Wales. But in 1892 the Devonshires left, the art treasures went back to Chatsworth, and the house became a lunatic asylum. In 1928 there was a danger of the house and park being sold for a housing development; but it was purchased by the Middlesex County Council, and then handed over to the Ministry of Works by deed of gift. It was, even, used as an emergency fire station during the Second World War. When the restoration by the Ministry of Works was begun, the two Wyatt wings were found to be so ruinous that they had to be torn down: so the villa today is that of Burlington's original conception.

The grounds are now maintained by the Borough, and very remarkable they are, with their fine avenues, their two obelisks, the artificial river with James Wyatt's classic bridge, the cascade, the rustic house and the Doric Temple. Together they give a complete picture of the landscape gardening of the time. There is here another splendid example of eighteenth-century taste—Inigo Jones' classic gateway, removed from Beaufort House in 1736. Chiselled on a stone tablet is Pope's memorial:

> *Inigo Jones put me together*
> *Sir Hans Sloane left me alone*
> *Burlington brought me thither*

It was in these gardens that young Joseph Paxton, Devonshire's protégé, worked on the erection of a large greenhouse which he had designed—a possible precursor of the Crystal Palace. But it is William Kent's influence that is paramount both in the house and the gardens. Kent was of humble origin, in his boyhood apprenticed to a coach builder. His promise as a painter was soon noticed. He was sent to Italy in 1709. There he studied, painted and acted as agent, buying for his patrons works of art, wine and books. He met Burlington in Italy in 1719 and came back to England with him. Burlington became his patron, introducing him at court, 'countenancing and promoting' him. He was well known and liked: Pope admired his wit, calling him 'The Signior'. He certainly ranks as one of Chiswick's most eminent worthies, for he lived in Chiswick House until his death in 1748, and is buried in the parish churchyard.

Outside Chiswick House a number of roads lead down to the Thames, and alongside it runs the Mall, the most attractive part of old Chiswick. There is not much of it—some half a mile—but into the Mall are gathered more good eighteenth-century houses than in any other part of Middlesex. All of them are elegant and well preserved, the most notable being Morton House, Strawberry House and Walpole House; the only oddity among these houses is Greenash, built in 1882 for Thornycroft the shipbuilder. It is pleasant (and reasonably safe, for there is little motor-traffic) to stroll along Chiswick Mall, the Thames on one side, unobscured by any embankment; the little island, Chiswick Eyot, retains some greenery which replaces the osiers which used to be grown there; small boats are moored along the banks. Many of the houses have a history. Walpole House was once the residence of Barbara Villiers, Countess of Castlemaine. A later occupant was Sir Herbert Beerbohm Tree. The antiquarians says that the house was the 'Miss Pinkerton's Academy' described by Thackeray in *Vanity Fair*; though this distinction is also claimed by Boston House in Chiswick Square nearby. There are one or two modern additions to the Mall—the houses in Eyot Green are pleasant and discreet. On the other hand the so-called 'Georgian mansions' at the Hammersmith end of the Mall are poor imitations of their well-proportioned neighbours. In Mawson Lane, just off the Mall, is a small inn, the *Fox and Hounds*, which was for three years the home of Alexander Pope, who lived there close to his friend Burlington before moving to Twickenham. At the far end of the Mall three nineteenth-century houses mark the site of the Chiswick Press; from here Charles Whittingham produced some of the finest typography of mid-Victorian times, in moderately priced books that are still highly esteemed. The press moved in 1875; but Whittingham's ideas inspired William Morris, who started his Kelmscott Press nearby in Hammersmith in 1891. The Mall ends abruptly, and warehouses loom by the river. Further round the curve of the river is Thornycroft's Quay, where the first fast steam launch was built in 1860: the quay is part of industrial rather than Middlesex history; the successors to the launch were the Royal Navy's 'torpedo-boats'.

Chiswick was once a town for fishermen, and Saint Nicholas, their patron, gives his name to the parish church, lying on a constricted green by the river. Only the tower remains of the fifteenth-century building, the main structure being of 1882; it is said that the bricks of the old church were pounded up to make mortar for the new. The interior of the church is plain and rather gloomy; many of the old monuments have been preserved, the oldest being that of Sir Thomas Chaloner of 1615. There has been a recent revival of the legend that

Oliver Cromwell's body lies in the vault under St. Nicholas, his coffin concealed near that of Lady Fauconberg, his third daughter. She was devoted to this church, worshipping there for five years, and giving the bells that hang in the tower. The Cromwell story remains a mystery—like other Cromwell legends of Middlesex. The bell-ringers performed one notable feat, commemorated by a plaque: a peal of grandsire triples, with 5,040 changes in just over three hours. The date was 1903; the year of the delayed coronation of Chiswick's most famous resident, King Edward VII.

The burial ground is more interesting than the church, for rarely can so many notable people be found in a small parish churchyard. Just by the side porch is a fine monument to William Hogarth, with a lengthy epitaph by David Garrick. There are other artists: Sir James Thornhill; James McNeill Whistler; and Philip de Louther-bourg, who painted magnificent scenery for Covent Garden. Garrick again provided a flowing epitaph for the actor, Charles Holland. Lord Burlington is buried here, and in his family tomb his architect friend Colen Campbell, William Kent who did so much in the design of Chiswick Villa, and his bricklayer Richard Wright. Whittingham of the Chiswick Press is here; while a plaque on the wall records the gift of 20 perches of land to the churchyard by the Duke of Devonshire. Many more of Chiswick's worthies are buried here, but the most unusual of them is Ugo Foscolo, the Italian critic and poet who, an exile, died in poverty in Turnham Green in 1827. His remains were removed to Santa Croce in Florence in 1871, but a plaque records the burial of the 'tired citizen-poet' in Chiswick, 'for ever held in grateful remembrance by the Italian nation'.

From Church Street up to Hogarth Lane is the centre of old Chiswick village, still a place of charm and comparative quiet. Pages Yard leads to Chiswick Square, a little enclave of four houses, the most handsome being Boston House (1780), with its handsome wrought-iron gates. Hogarth Lane is no longer a lane, but a section of the Great West Road, teeming with traffic day and night, for it is on the direct route to Heathrow Airport. To reach Chiswick Square one has to dive into an underground passage: the exit from another passage leads to a narrow strip of pavement, on which lie the gates of

Hogarth House. On one side is a laundry, on the other the vast bulk of the Reckitt Colman factory. It is a miracle that Hogarth House is here at all, for it was bomb damaged in the Second World War. To the credit of the Chiswick and Middlesex councils it was restored and reopened in 1951. Most of its small garden survives and in its centre is the mulberry tree Hogarth used to sit under; struck by lightning in Hogarth's time, damaged by the bomb in 1940, it yet bore a few mulberries (after some coaxing by an expert from Kew) in 1951. This 'little country box by the Thames' is where William Hogarth lived from 1749-1764. Twenty years later the little box was derelict; it was only in 1902 that it was bought by private generosity and became the Hogarth Museum. It is an unpretentious house, nicely kept inside, with five rooms whose walls are full of Hogarth's engravings: there are also a few curiosities of the artist's time. But the museum was deserted on the day I was there: and (from a scrutiny of the visitor's book) it is by no means frequented. The reason, I suppose, is its inaccessibility. At least it *is* here and it *is* preserved; and there can be no finer display of Hogarth's engraved work anywhere else in Britain.

It is the Thames that gives Chiswick most of its charm: away from it there is a mass of housing, varied in character, but seldom downright ugly. In the curve of the river past the Mall are acres of green playing fields, the principal of them being Duke's Meadows. The towpath alongside the river is a favourite place for watching the Oxford and Cambridge boat race. The Great Chertsey Road cuts across the meadows to Chiswick Bridge; along Harlington Road and through the suburb of Grove Park lies Chiswick's second village— Strand-on-the-Green. It remains a village because nobody has been able to interfere with it; its main street a narrow walk alongside the Thames, with no motor traffic. For some half a mile there is as delightful a group of houses as one can find anywhere on Thameside. They are less pretentious than in the Mall: most of them have been fisherman's cottages, refurbished, repointed and modernised. Only two of them, Springfield House and Zoffany House, are of real architectural interest. In the latter lived John Zoffany, the Academician, from 1780 to 1810. He excelled in portraits and 'conversation pieces'.

There is a delightful portrait by him, of Mrs. John Sharp, a musician's wife, who was his neighbour. From here he must have gone to paint his *Last Supper*: the models for the Apostles were Strand-on-the-Green fishermen, St. Peter, the portrait of the artist. The picture, once in St. George's Church Brentford, has been moved several times, and is still in Brentford; but as the two churches are closed, I found it difficult to trace. The modern houses at Strand-on-the-Green combine well with the older ones. 'Number Nought' is very handsome, with its well designed railings protecting it from the passer-by. Magnolia Court, though a twentieth-century block of flats, has weatherboarding similar to its neighbours. There are three village inns, the *Bull*, the *Bell and Crown* and the *City Barge*. The last is so named because the Lord Mayor's decorative barge, the *Maria Wood*, was for long moored here. There is little to mar the picturesque village except a massive iron railway bridge which crosses high above the Thames. Life must occasionally be uncomfortable, for the strand is frequently flooded. Strand-on-the-Green's only other worthy was Joe Miller, the famous comedian of the eighteenth century, famous for his *Jest-book*, staple fare for comedians even in this century; but not written by Miller but by one John Modley. The charming Strand-on-the-Green ends in a sick joke: warehouses, an appalling brick laundry, a huge pub, and the beginnings of Brentford.

The Thames-side entrance to Brentford is anything but handsome: a high yellow brick wall that extends for hundreds of yards alongside the river. Opposite is the Kew Bridge Water Works with its 'minaret' tower. Then comes an enormous gas-holder sheathed in wood, the tall cylinder visible from many of the heights of Middlesex. The water works was established in 1835 by the Grand Junction Canal authority. Its entrance gates are forbidding, but the amateur of industrial archaeology may care to enter them, for in one of the buildings is a great pumping engine of 1820 made by Boulton and Watt. Next to the water works is a church and a small schoolhouse of the late eighteenth century where Sarah Trimmer taught Sunday school. But the school is empty, and St. George's no longer a church. Instead, it has become the British Piano and Musical Museum, one of the most curious and engaging (and probably the least known) of all

London's museums. I promised Mr. Holland the director that my stay would be brief, as I was visiting on a weekday, outside regular hours; but there was so much to see, and so great was the director's enthusiasm, that I was there for well over an hour. A few church fittings remain in the entrance porch, but the body of the church has been cleared to house dozens of musical instruments. They are mostly pianos, of all shapes and sizes: but among them are organs (straightforward or mechanical), a nickleodion, an 'orchestrion', and many varieties of musical boxes. From the roof (which leaks badly) hang vast sheets of polythene! beneath it are 50 tons of instruments, all kept in working order by the care and attention of Mr. Holland and his faithful assistant Miss Brasher. Having been solemnly enjoined not to call them 'pianolas', but 'reproducing pianos', I was given a demonstration. An elegant Victorian Erard (on which Mendelssohn had played) gave out a song without words; a square little musical box wheezed *A cottage by the stream*; a fine Bechstein, equipped with a roll made by Rubinstein, played Granados; I heard, on the mechanical organ, a Thalben Ball rendering of the *Trumpet Voluntary*. The grand climax came with the orchestrion which, equipped with horns, trumpets and organ pipes, blared out a Sousa march. The larger mechanical instruments bristle with gauges, recording knots, miles per hour, or volts (anything as long as they work). It is all odd, entertaining, instructive and very evidently a labour of love. This unique museum is open on Saturday and Sunday afternoons from March to November. It may be moved in the general clearance in this part of Brentford: it certainly must not be dispersed, or vanish.

The general clearance is very evident in the High Street. Rows of Victorian terrace houses have been removed; the few remnants remaining are shabby and unsavoury-looking. Open spaces are covered with rubble. In the distance, by the motorway, five vast 22-storey blocks of flats have risen, to house 4,000 people, perhaps the total population of the cleared area. The old shops have closed, or are decaying. A few places such as *The Bee Hive* and the *Red Lion* hang on to some life. A Victorian mansion converted into a factory is surrounded by rusty scrap; near it a dusty-looking block of municipal dwellings stands; opposite, a new five-storey block of flats looks dis-

22 Strawberry Hill, Twickenham

23 Strawberry Hill: the Library

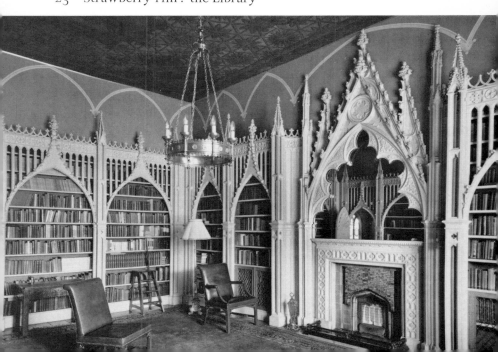

24 York House, Twickenham

25 Marble Hill House, Twickenham

dainful in these surroundings. The parish church of St. Lawrence is closed except for weddings and christenings. The Zoffany painting is supposed to be in this church : but each time I visited it the church was closed. There is another church and graveyard on the opposite side of the High Street : it is firmly closed, with not even a notice board to reveal its name. Further on a new shopping centre has risen. Most of this part of Brentford is in a state of transition : a £50,000,000 building scheme will soon bring it into the twentieth century.

Towards the river, down Dock Road, King's Arms Alley, Ferry Lane and Catherine Wheel Yard, the remains of Brentford's shipping yards and traffic on the Thames may be found. Ferry Lane is the old ford where the river Brent enters the Thames. At the end of the lane is a column, heavily inscribed. The first inscription reads 'In 54 B.C., at this ancient fortified ford of the Thames, the British tribesmen under Casivellaunus bravely opposed Julius Caesar'. (In 1909 some ancient palisades were indeed recovered from the Thames near here.) The column also records that Offa held a council of the Church here in A.D. 780 and commemorates the defeat of the Danes by Edmond Ironside in 1016. There is a fourth inscription recording the battle of Brentford in 1642, when the Royalists defeated the Parliamentarians, and plundered the village, going on the next day to a defeat at Turnham Green. Down Dock Road is Brentside Dock, with a lock on this backwater of the Thames, an entrance to the Grand Union Canal. There is a little shipyard here, with a rusty hull on the stocks. Barges are repaired and painted, and huge piles of waste paper and wood pulp, unloaded from the barges, lie on the quay. Across the water are the ruins of a vast railway depot, behind them the trees of Kew Gardens. In the maze of alleys and sheds on the Middlesex side there are still a few cottages. The whole area is soon to be redeveloped, with a marina, housing (without tower blocks), and a complete remodelling of the landscape.

Behind the new developments in Brentford High Street a few places remain as a reminder that Brentford was once the county town of Middlesex. There is the old Market Square and a Magistrate's Court. Brentford Market after a long period of decay is flourishing again—the local guide calls it 'West London's Covent Garden'. The best domestic architecture is to be found in The Butts, where some good eighteenth-century houses are grouped round a rectangular open space. It is a quiet place: once, no doubt, grass, but now asphalted. The name suggests archery, but this was formerly the site of the hustings for Middlesex elections, which were notoriously rowdy and ill-conducted. In 1769, when John Wilkes was standing, the mob destroyed the poll-books, and a man was killed in the ensuing riot. There is nothing here to remind the visitor of the 'continued scene of riot, disorder and tumult' (as the *Annual Register* called it) that once was—not even a plaque. Up the road called Half Acre, under the pylons of the motorway, are the sedate houses of New Brentford. And here is one of Brentford's finest old houses, Boston Manor of 1623, a good Jacobean mansion of three storeys, set in a neat park with a small lake. James Clitheroe, once a Lord Mayor of London, owned it in 1670. It has undergone many vicissitudes since then, including bomb-damage during the last war. Now with its fine plaster ceilings and staircase restored it belongs to the National Institute of Housecraft, who use it as a training centre. It is not open to the public, but organised parties are shown round during the summer months.

The most magnificent house in the neighbourhood, however, is Syon, situated in a great park which follows the curve of the Thames. The place has a tremendous history, extending over 500 years. Syon Abbey was once a Bridgettine monastery: in 1547 after the dissolution of the monasteries, the abbey and park were granted to the Duke of Somerset, Protector of the Realm. Here he built a house, and its shell forms the core of the present building. Somerset, too, started the gardens here, and the old mulberry trees (which still bear fruit) were planted by Turner, his house physician. The estate eventually came to the Dukes of Northumberland, and Henry Percy the scholar-philosopher, the 'wizard-earl', lived here, accumulating a great library. It was Sir Hugh Smithson, created First Duke of Northumberland in 1766, who engaged Robert Adam to bring the house to its present glory.

And glorious it is, though plain, even grim, in its exterior. At the

entrance the Percy lion proudly stands above the archway : inside,
as the guide-book says 'the full grandeur of Adam's conception is
realised.' It would be useless to describe Syon in detail: it must be
seen. The Great Hall with its marble and its statuary, the Ante-room
blazing in red, blue and gold, the drawing room, the furniture, ornaments and pictures: all are rich, varied and fascinating. The Long
Gallery, in spite of its size (136 by 14 feet), is perfect in proportion.
Adam designed it for the ladies and it was 'finished in a style to
afford variety and amusement'. It is typical of the care with which
Syon is maintained that Adam's original design for the carpet in the
Long Gallery has recently been manufactured and laid, making the
gallery even more splendid. Above all Syon is lived in, and looks like
a home.

The story of the house and its possessions is told in an excellent
handbook published by the Syon House Estate. The park, originally
laid out by 'Capability' Brown, has been well maintained throughout
the years. There has been some criticism of the owners because in
1965 55 acres of the park were hived off to form the Gardening
Centre, a commercial undertaking. It has even been called 'an odious
act of vandalism'. Certainly the new buildings of the Centre form
an extraordinary contrast with the sober façade of the great house :
the red bricks have not yet mellowed; there is too much gravel and
car park, too many notices. But the centre blazes with flowers, and
its exhibits are interesting. To sit and have tea outside the teahouse
on a sunny afternoon, admiring the lawns, the willow-trees, the
ornamental lake and Fowler's 'Great Conservatory' is a great pleasure. I give all praise to those who arranged, on the lawns, an exhibition of sculpture by Barbara Hepworth, in a setting that displays
their austere beauty.

> *Here in the silent pleasances of Syon*
> *The centuries are gathered up in one*

wrote Adrian Bury. The pleasances are silent no longer, but thousands more may enjoy them; while the twentieth century has been
added to the others in Syon's rich history. Syon remains as the most
splendid house in Middlesex.

Syon House lies within the old borough of Isleworth, and away from London Road, teeming with traffic, down Church Road and alongside the river, are the remains of Isleworth village. A few pleasant old houses lie along the way. Syon Park Lodge, now used as offices, was once a school, among its pupils Shelley and John Rennie, the great engineer. Isleworth Draw Dock has still the air of a riverside village, with a few barges and small boats drawn up on the strand. Its inn, *The London Apprentice*, has some antiquity, and is well known for its food. There is a considerable island, Isleworth Ait, in the river, and a mill stream, with the curiously named Mill Plat, a narrow street, alongside it. The Mill has long ago vanished: but the Plat with Upper and Lower Square formed the centre of old Isleworth, and to get into or out of it, water had always to be crossed, so much did the Thames and its tributaries permeate the place. The parish church, All Saints, stands on the river bank. Only the 1450 tower now remains: the rest of the church was burnt down, by accident, in 1950. Around the tower has risen a new church, uncompromisingly of this century, built of wood and darkly burnt brick, a place which has the feeling of Gothic without imitating it. Inside, the place is full of drama: the roof is inverted, supported by massive wood columns: the high narrow windows have colourful stained glass by Michael Blee. The body of the church is on several levels, with a central altar. This is, certainly, one of the most interesting Anglican churches of this century in Middlesex.

The village in which the church stands was in the last century a popular Thames-side dwelling place. Earlier, R. B. Sheridan lived here, later, the Duchess of Kendal. J. M. W. Turner lived here as a boy with his uncle and here is supposed to have begun to draw. Isleworth had its small industries, a brass and copper mill, and there was a corn-mill, an early effort at cooperation owned by 120 members of the 'Good Intent Society'. Berry Wharf was busy with barges loading up with gunpowder from the mills in Hanworth, a few miles away. But Isleworth was chiefly known for its market-gardens: the oldest inhabitants tell of an invasion of women from Shropshire who helped with the apple-picking. Not far from the village, in Twickenham Road, a plaque commemorates one world-famous figure—Vincent van Gogh. He stayed here in 1876, giving religious instruction in Sunday schools, living with a Mr. Jones, and receiving only pocket money. His letters to his brother Theo speak of the charm of the riverside and the great parks. But he had not yet become an artist, and there are no sketches of Isleworth in the letters.

Away from its village, Isleworth becomes crowded with housing, mostly mid-Victorian in the Spring Grove area. There is a large and developing Polytechnic, the central part of which was once the mansion of Andrew Pears, the Victorian soap-magnate. The Teacher's Training College in Borough Road was once famous as the International College, two of whose pupils were Maurice Hewlett, the novelist, and Frederick Delius, the composer. This part of Isleworth is in a state of upheaval, with flats and shops replacing the mansions. The products of such upheavals are evident in Crowther's Yard in London Road, which advertises 'ten acres of antiques'; here one can buy anything from an old gable to a garden ornament. London Road is busy: the Great West Road which runs through Osterley is thronged with motor traffic, and in the latter the chief feature is factories—the greatest concentration in Middlesex outside Park Royal. They are of all shapes and sizes, the most grandiose being the Gillette factory, designed by Sir Banister Fletcher, with its 150-foot clock tower. None of them is an architectural masterpiece: but all are neat, clean and smokeless; many are embellished with lawns and trees, many floodlit by night. There is one half-mile section of the road which, towards Christmas-tide, is fringed by illuminated Christmas trees—a pleasant sight in the winter dusk. There are three smaller modern buildings among the factories that have some style, amid much mediocrity; the Osterley Motel is new, plain and inviting. The tube station is typical London Transport architecture with a rather charming tower above its booking-hall. The Osterley branch library, too, is neat and attractive.

There are many green spaces behind the factories. The chief of them is Osterley Park, with its great house, originally built by Sir Thomas Gresham, the banker, in 1577. It was rebuilt by another banker, Sir Francis Child, between 1760 and 1780, his architects being Sir William Chambers and Robert Adam. The house eventually descended to the Earls of Jersey, and was given to the National Trust in 1949. The park is a fine one, with many noble trees; the original Elizabethan stables have been preserved; and the ornamental lake (which Horace Walpole admired so much) retains its charm. The only remaining parts of the Child mansion are the four square towers at the corners. These were refaced by Adam, and two of them flank the great symmetrical classical façade, its central feature a tremendous portico with six Ionic columns, leading to a courtyard. The entrance is imposing, but must surely have been draughty and inconvenient for Child's guests. Walpole called Syon a 'palace of palaces'—and most aptly. The entrance hall is cool, chaste, classical, with two staircases leading to the state apartments on the first floor. These are very fine, richly decorated with tapestries, and ceiling paintings by Zucchi. There is a delightful library, and a state bed-chamber of surpassing grandeur. Much of Adam's original furniture is displayed. The one failure is the Etruscan Room: one of Adam's experiments, which Horace Walpole thought, on his second visit, to be 'a profound tumble into the bathos'.

Osterley House is magnificent, and well maintained by the Ministry of Works. The final impression one takes away is one of ostentation, however: Syon is still a home, Osterley more of a museum. Gresham, its original owner, was ostentatious. When Elizabeth I visited him here in 1576 she criticised the proportions of the courtyard. So Sir Thomas, overnight, had a wall built down the middle of it: 'It was questionable,' wrote Thomas Fuller, 'whether the Queen was more contented with the conformity to her fancy, or more pleased with the surprise and the sudden performance thereof.' There were several owners after Gresham, among them Coke, the Lord Chief Justice, and Sir William Waller, the Parliamentarian general, who died here in 1668. It was a granddaughter of the Child family who inherited the estate and married the fifth Earl of Jersey. This great house has had many vicissitudes since then, including a damaging fire in 1879. One of the most bizarre periods of Osterley's history lasted for a few months in 1940. The Earl of Jersey offered it to Edward Hulton as a training centre for the Home Guard. Within a few weeks 250 enthusiasts were installed, with Tom Wintringham, the expert in guerilla warfare as chief instructor. Barricades and tank-traps were made in the park, home-made dynamite brewed up in the kitchens, Molotov cocktails made. The War Office authorities frowned on these irregularities, and the school soon closed down; but there was thereafter a more realistic attitude to Home Guard training.

The M.4 motorway cuts across Osterley Park. On one side of it is Southall, now part of the borough of Ealing, a place that has grown up since 1839, when the Great Western Railway came there. It is a bustling twentieth-century place, where much 'processed food' is made, in factories manned by Pakistanis. There are no problems of race relations with this mild mannered people, except that it is now difficult to see anything but Indian films in the cinemas. Southall has some connections with history, and its 1581 manor house, well preserved, stands on the Green. The market still held in Southall was granted by a charter of 1698.

On the other side of the motorway is Heston, the former companion to Isleworth in the old system of London boroughs. In Elizabethan times it was rich farm land, famous for its wheat. In the nineteenth century it became a centre for brickmaking, and Robbins records that much of London was built of Heston brown stocks. Here again, little of the past remains. St. Leonards, the parish church, was rebuilt in 1856, but the fifteenth-century tower remains (like many others in Middlesex). There is, however, in the Victorian structure, one important monument by Adam and Van Gelder—to Robert Child of Osterley Park, son of the original owner. The rest of Heston seems to have nothing but the usual features of a London suburb: houses, schools, factories, swimming bath and some public buildings. But in a corner of the borough not far from the Bath Road is a circle of houses named after pioneers of aviation—Brabazon, Bleriot, Sopwith, Cobham, Johnson, Whittle, and Alcock. They are a reminder that Heston Airport was once internationally famous. Little remains now except a tower and a few outbuildings. There is, however, one splendid modern building, the B.E.A. Training School: eight storeys of flats, six storeys of training centre: a poised and satisfying piece of modern architecture. Otherwise, there are only bleak looking fields to remind us that this was an international aerodrome extensively used for official purposes. Its last great event was on September 30th, 1938 when, back from Munich, Neville Chamberlain came from his plane, clutching a piece of paper, and calling to the crowd 'I've got it!'

CHAPTER TEN

Riverside Towns and Villages

'Hounslow Heath', wrote Cobbett in *Rural Rides*, 'is a sample of all that is bad in soil, and villainous in look.' Today the open spaces and fields of Hounslow, Feltham and Hanworth have the same characteristics Cobbett noticed: a thin layer of soil over a great deal of gravel, in a flat featureless plain. In Elizabethan times Hounslow was celebrated for its wheat. All the farms have gone today. Even in 1816 the High Street was notorious for its 'immense tide of road traffic'; today it seethes with buses, motor-cars, it is full of pedestrian crossings and traffic lights, with hundreds of shoppers. The civic centre, with its Town Hall, Baths and Library (all of 1905), is no longer a 'centre', but merely a series of departmental offices in the London borough of Heston and Isleworth. The few traces of history to be found are in the open spaces of Hanworth Park and Hounslow Heath.

Hounslow Heath, once an immense tract of 6,000 acres, has grown much smaller during the last century. In the eighteenth century it was a dangerous place, frequented by highwaymen, and famed for its array of gibbets on which the unsuccessful robbers were strung up. Well into the nineteenth century coachmen were armed against the highwaymen. They were not all professionals, however: buried in East Bedfont church is the amateur William Langley, who in 1768 held up a coach in Bedfont Lane. He was shot on the spot. Shooting and explosions seem to have been part of the daily life of Hounslow Heath for hundreds of years, for it has for long been a resort of the military. As far back as 1267, the Earl of Gloucester arrayed an army of Londoners here to give battle against King Henry III. The Heath was the Royalist encampment before the battle of Brentford: 20,000 men of the Parliamentarian army assembled there in 1647. Then the temporary camp became a permanent one, with cavalry barracks, in 1875. Large portions of the heath have been virtually closed to the public for over a century. Somewhere in the military area is a monumental tablet commemorating one remarkable achievement; the beginning of the Ordnance Survey. The first triangulation point was set up on the heath by General William Roy in 1783. It is reported that the Army will soon leave Hounslow. Already parts of the perimeter are being surrounded by houses and tall blocks of flats, and there will be an estate to house 2,000 families, with 130 acres of open space. Allied to the military occupation were the celebrated 'powder mills' at North Feltham near Baber Bridge. It is said that some of the first gunpowder made in England was manufactured here. It was chancy stuff: the explosions, which occurred every few months, terrified Middlesex residents for two centuries. Horace Walpole complained about one which in 1772, damaged parts of his house at Strawberry Hill. There is still an Ordnance Depot on the map of Hounslow, but it is inconspicuous, and silent.

Hounslow's only other considerable open space is Hanworth Park, formerly an aerodrome, now used as a sport's ground. It is a place of some history, for Henry VIII had a hunting lodge here: the lodge was eventually settled on Katherine Parr. Elizabeth I, while a princess, lived there and is said to have revisited the park and hunted in it after her accession to the throne. The lodge burned down in 1797, and the only relics that remain are a few plaques embodied in the gateway of Tudor Court, a block of flats. A large nineteenth-century house is in the centre of the park, surrounded by trees, and surrounded again by massive palings; its chief feature is a profusion of Victorian iron porches and balconies. Once a hotel, it is now a home for old people. The park was once an aerodrome, and the *Graf Zeppelin* landed there. The hangars at the side of the park are now empty: appropriately enough, however, there were aircraft about— models controlled by a swarm of small boys dashing around in the distance. The park, a very large place, must be pleasant in the summer, and the Council have built a handsome open air swimming pool in one corner of it. The aeroplane, however, still dominates Hanworth, for it is on the flight path to Heathrow, only two miles away. Fagg's Road, which leads out of Harlington Road, is the entry to a trading estate of buildings associated with Heathrow, including the Hovercraft Unit of the Ministry of Technology; while by Fagg's Bridge are the extraordinary long buildings of the Ship Hydrodynamics Section of the National Physical Laboratory.

Here we are in Feltham, the flattest and most bleak area of the county. In its upper part the chief feature is a huge railway marshalling yard surrounded by mediocre housing and small factories, with the River Crane wandering through behind them. The real village is Lower Feltham: approaching it down Bedfont Lane is a dispiriting experience. The landscape is level and waterlogged; here and there vast yellow machines scoop out gravel: the pits thus formed fill up with water. The pits are eventually filled again with rubbish. There are a few stray cottages. The only considerable building is a large Borstal institution of Victorian times. Lower Feltham village is a little triangle of houses near the Ashford Road, with a few cottages and St. Dunstan's church. The church is small and unpretentious, with arched windows and a small spire. The church is remarkable for its sheer simplicity: apparently there was no money to spare for ornamentation in the rebuilding of 1802. The result is a charming austerity. The base of the wooden gallery records, in a lively Victorian script, the names of the vicar and churchwardens at the time of a later restoration: tablets on the walls are memorials to a few village worthies. There is little decorative work, save for a fine window of pale blue glass. There is one modern tablet, to William Barclay Squire the Victorian musicologist, famous for his work on English madrigals, and his catalogue of early music in the British Museum. The burial ground outside is overgrown; its only notable tomb that of W. W. Ryland, an engraver whose talents were too diverse—he 'forged and uttered' bills of exchange and was hanged for it in 1783. The only other celebrity of Feltham was Frances Maria Kelly, the actress, celebrated in verse by Charles Lamb; she lived here to the age of 90, dying in 1883. But nobody could tell me where her dwelling, Rose Cottage, might be. There is very little of the old village left: one or two Victorian cottages by the church, a barn-like building which may be the manor house described by Pevsner, but much altered; and the Victorian Inn the *Rose and Crown*, now shuttered, dark and falling to pieces. There is an air of melancholy about Lower Feltham.

The next village (or small town) is Ashford. Its two churches are uninteresting, its Welsh school a great pile of Victorian Gothic; and the farm in Clockhouse Lane seems to have disappeared. Ashford, with its neighbours the Bedfonts, Stanwell and Staines were all parts of Middlesex. Since 1965 they have been in Surrey. The passer-by does not notice any change; nor do most of the inhabitants, for few of them that I talked to would admit that they were in any place but Middlesex. It is even more difficult to find out in which borough one is; and travelling up Clockhouse Lane towards East Bedfont, only the map gives the evidence that this village is on the border of the London Borough of Hounslow. Tucked away in a triangle between the Staines and Great South West roads, it is still a village with a green, a sixteenth-century manor, Tudor and Georgian houses and a fine old church. There was, too, a typical village scene on the day I visited East Bedfont, with the church bells pealing for a wedding, the guests moving across the road to the church hall. St. Mary the Virgin's Church is very mixed in style, with a curious wooden spire. The church, founded in 1150, has a few remains of Norman architecture, the chief being the zigzag chancel arch, said to be the only one in Middlesex. There are two thirteenth-century wall paintings of the Last Judgment, discovered during a restoration in 1865. Other curiosities are a carved Flemish relief of the fifteenth century and a darkly embrowned painted monument of 1640. The chief memorials are to the Page and the Sherborne families, both of them occupants of Pates Manor House, near the church. There is a neat little balcony, its front panel setting out the commandments in an elegant script. All in all, this is one of the more interesting parish churches of the county, and the legends that have grown about it are as interesting as the architecture. Up to 1940 the church was famous for its topiary-work: two large yew-trees in the churchyard have been cut into fantastic shapes, said to be two peacocks. Engravings and photographs through two centuries show the trees, which were almost as high as the church. Thomas Hood, in his poem *The Two Peacocks of Bedfont*, connected the yews with two maiden ladies who refused many offers of marriage; another chronicler writes that the birds were fighting cocks. Whatever they were, the church records show payments for cutting the yews from 1751 onwards.

The church records of St. Mary reveal much about the life of the village in the eighteenth and nineteenth centuries. There is the story of William Langley, the amateurish highwayman, buried under a plain stone in the churchyard. His burial cost the churchwardens £1. 8s. 6d. but they recovered £1. 9s. 8d. for his 'clos and pistoles and things'. There are three entries for Bedfont men 'blown up at the powder mills'. Burlington House, next to the church, is a well-preserved eighteenth-century building.

West Bedfont and Stanwell are in effect one community; here we are in Staines, formerly an urban district of Middlesex. Stanwell's chief feature is water—3,300 million gallons of it, contained in the King George VI and Staines reservoirs, the latter so huge that a breakwater has been built across it to prevent wave movements. Stanwell Moor Road, which runs for a mile between the two reservoirs, is the most featureless road in the county, running through grassy banks some 20 feet high, their only adornment a few frail saplings, all with wire fencing. The surrealist landscape looks like a painting by Magritte. The reservoir water is not visible, and is more familiar to the air-traveller than the motorist. These great sheets of water form two of the largest bird sanctuaries in the county. Enormous numbers of birds come here, chiefly gulls: movements of over 25,000 a day have been recorded. But many other species of water bird—duck, tern and mallards—regularly are listed in the *London Bird report*.

The Moor Road leads to Stanwell, a flourishing little community, once one of the most isolated of Middlesex villages. It is an old place, recorded in Domesday. The manor was large and included several other villages. It was appropriated by Henry VIII from its owner, Lord Windsor. It is the Knyvett family, who were granted the manor in 1603 by James I, that can be traced in Stanwell today.

Thomas, Lord Knyvett was a great man in his day, guardian of the King's daughter Princess Mary, who died in Stanwell in 1607. Thomas Knyvett was a justice of the peace for Westminster, and it was he who discovered the Gunpowder Plot in 1605. Stanwell Place is a Georgian house which replaced the old manor, and its imposing entrance is outside the village. Knyvett's 'Free School' of 1624 still stands: a handsome brick structure, still in use as a primary school. A few Georgian houses remain in Stanwell, and one farm survives away from the built-up area. The chief attraction, however, is the pleasant village green and the church of St. Mary, with its tower, of the thirteenth and fourteenth century, which seems to lean on one side.

The interior of the church is lofty and has a fine fifteenth-century clerestory. The roof of the aisle has been replaced, but the finely carved fourteenth-century corbels are still there—kings, queens, knights and pilgrims. I was lucky to get into the church, which is generally kept closed. I saw Nicholas Stone's splendid marble tomb of Lord and Lady Knyvett, the brass of Nicholas Thorp of 1408, and high in the wall, the 'Easter sepulchre', a memorial to Thomas Windsor, the original Lord of the manor. There is a two manual organ, 150 years old. In the loft of the belltower are a number of plaques, each commemorating 5,040 changes of 'plain bob minor', 'surprise minor' or 'primrose surprise minor', each rung for some special occasion. Stanwell has a long tradition of campanology, and the bell captain is as proud of his team as the organist of his choir. The old custom of ringing handbells for the Christmas festival is still kept up, and the team have summer tours to bell-towers in the home counties. Climbing up another ladder, I was allowed to see the bells hanging in their massive cage. I inspected the primitive mechanism of the 20-year-old clock, which strikes the hours on the largest bell. Finally, after another dizzying climb under the ancient beams of the tower, I was able to look out—at the runway of Heathrow, half a mile away.

Stanwell is a place of some tradition, but many of the acres around it were, up to 1900, merely a portion of Hounslow Heath. The 'barren heath' aspect persists as one travels up Stanwell Moor Road through flat land interlaced with artificial and natural rivers, the Longford, the Wyrardsbury and the Colne. One or two farms survive in this corner of the county, where Middlesex meets Buckinghamshire. The chief influence on the landscape is Heathrow, which, though its runways are not expanding, is extending its periphery, with small factories, warehouses and trading estates building up in the country lanes. Longford is simply a name on the map—Poyle village merely a row of houses which the motorist passes through on his way to the next county. But Poyle has some connection with history. There is nothing to single out Lawn Cottage from the row of houses; but there lived Richard Cox, who bred in his garden the most famous of England's apples—Cox's Orange Pippin. Poyle Manor (what remains of it) lies down a muddy lane; the lord of the manor was Nicholas Hilliard, our greatest miniature painter, who was granted the manor and other properties (worth £40 per annum) by Elizabeth I, for designing and executing the Queen's second great seal. Here in Poyle and Colnbrook is the division between Middlesex and Buckingham, the 'boundary bridge' of 1770 marking the divide, with a small portion of Colnbrook in Middlesex. There are a few cottages along the roadside, and two eighteenth-century inns, the *White Hart* and *Star and Garter*. Altogether there are four inns in this small village: a reminder of coaching days when Colnbrook was a busy staging post on the West Road. The chief building is a large white L-shaped house with black timbers. An archway leads to a courtyard and an old barn. Inside, all is clean and neat, sparkling with new paint; this sixteenth-century building has been transformed into a series of flatlets, occupied by air-hostesses and other employees of the air lines. The Royal Commission refers to it as the building 'called' King John's Palace, and gives its date as sixteenth or early seventeenth century. But the village legend persists—this was the house where King John stayed on his way to Runnymede before signing Magna Carta in 1312. And why not? It is less than five miles from Colnbrook.

Poyle Lane and Moor Lane lead southward towards Staines, the border town of Middlesex. The landscape is again flat, the King George VI reservoir on one side, great lakes (a proposed reservoir) on the other. This is Staines Moor. There is one farm, and a quiet little community at Yeoveney, but as soon at the by-pass road we are in Staines, and all is traffic and bustle. The remains of the older town are clustered around Staines Bridge, for centuries the most important in the county. The present bridge—George Rennie's structure of 1832—is the fourth on the site and is still handsome in spite of a modern widening. The walls of the brewery beside the bridge lead into Church Street, the oldest and most pleasant part of the town, with a number of eighteenth-century houses. Here and in Binbury Row and Vicarage Road, are the remains of the old village of Staines. St. Mary's church is undistinguished, having been rebuilt in 1828. Its best feature is a square tower on which a tablet boldly proclaims 'built by Inigo Jones in 1631'. None of the architectural authorities seem to credit this statement; nor can the date of A.D. 651 for the foundation of the church find much support. Even the name 'Stana' makes its first documentary appearance only in 969. Staines is undoubtedly an ancient place, for the archaeologists identify it with the Roman settlement *Ad Pontes*, and the settlement stood at the junction of the Roman road *Segontiacum*. The chief relic of the older days of Staines is to be found in the meadows alongside the river Thames, where in a playing field stands the London Stone. This sixteenth-century stone is set on a small plinth and represents the boundary of the jurisdiction of the city of London over the river, and the division between the Upper and Lower Thames. The stone is neglected: green with lichen, its inscription 'God preserve ye Citty' is almost unreadable. Various Lord Mayors have had their names inscribed below the plinth—the last was Sir Rupert de la Bere in 1957.

Away from the bridge and through the shopping centre is Thames Street and the road to Laleham and Chertsey. The Thames is the border of Middlesex: and the road to Laleham is surely one of the most pleasant in the county, comparatively unfrequented, with the river flowing placidly on one side. There are a few modern houses on the bank. Between them are glimpses of the water, a few houseboats, the occasional swan. This was the reach of the river that Thomas Arnold loved, when he lived here in 1819. 'I have always a

resource at hand in the bank of the river,' he wrote, 'which though it be perfectly flat has great charm from its entire loneliness.... None of that stir of boats and barges upon it.' Certainly less lonely than in Arnold's day, there is still a good deal of charm left here. Laleham itself is a little isolated, just away from the river, and some half a mile from another great reservoir, the Queen Mary, the latest to be completed. This vast artificial lake (4,400 million gallons of it) seems with its high grassed banks to sterilise the country around it. Apart from its size it is notable for being the one place in Middlesex where the bird watcher can expect to find herons nesting and breeding: 35 of them have been recorded.

Laleham is a serene little place, with little scope for expansion. There are some half-dozen avenues of houses on the riverside away from the main road, two farms, a little recreation ground and a school. The only large house is Laleham Abbey, now the community of Saint Peter the Apostle. It is a fine building of 1802, very plain, with massive Doric portico, set in a fine park with noble trees; it was formerly the home of Lord Lucan, the general who commanded the cavalry at Balaclava. Abbey Drive, which curves round a corner of the park, is full of fine houses, with a delightful thatched cottage. All Saints Church is a mixture of many centuries, with a rather uncompromising Georgian tower. Within are Norman arcades, a chapel named after the Lucans, and a few minor memorials. There are only two decorations in the church. One is a great painting of Christ on the sea with Peter; so the authorities say, but its details can scarcely be seen, the varnish is so embrowned. The other decoration is a modern stained-glass window, glowing with remarkable colour, showing St. Christopher with the child Jesus on his shoulder and at the side, singers and fishermen with St. Eustace and St. Cecilia. The window was designed by W. A. Geddes, and was placed there as a memorial to P. G. Balfour, the organist, who died at his console at the end of an evening service in January 1925. It is, in fact, the men who served Laleham church who are more interesting than its fabric. Thomas Arnold started his first private school here in 1819, and his community became famous before his removal to Rugby in 1828. Six of his nine children were born in Laleham. Matthew Arnold was born here in 1822, came to his uncle, John Buckland's preparatory school, and constantly revisited Laleham in his later life; he and three of his sons are buried in All Saints churchyard, and the grave is still cared for by the pupils of a school named after him. Buckland's preparatory school, run on strict church principles, became one of the most famous in Victorian England, turning out muscular Christians for 34 years. A Victorian atmosphere persists in Laleham village. It is a backwater and a very pleasant one.

Some two miles away from Laleham, and past Chertsey Bridge, the Thames twists and curves through Chertsey Meads, round Pharoah's island, and down to Shepperton Lock. This is one of the most picturesque parts of the river, where the river Wey joins the Thames. Shepperton is one of the best of the Thames-side towns; it seems to lack a modern shopping centre and is all the better for it. The two adjacent villages of Upper and Lower Halliford are a discreet mixture of old and new. Chertsey Road is indeed busy with motor-traffic. There are ominous looking dotted lines on the newer maps, indicating that a motorway may soon slash its way through this quiet place; in the meantime the visitor may enjoy the unique Shepperton Square on the banks of the river. 'Here,' writes Pevsner, 'is one of the most perfect village pictures Middlesex has to offer.'

Pevsner wrote these words 20 years ago, but the square is still charming in spite of a garish petrol station and a brash restaurant. The grouping is perfect, with rectory, church, two hotels, an inn and half-a-dozen old houses. The rectory is a fine old building, in seven bays, dating from 1700; its large hall is believed to be of 1485. Set in an attractive garden with a lawn 200 years old, the rectory has been divided into a parsonage house and two flats, but remains unspoilt—surely the finest of its kind in Middlesex. St. Nicholas church has no architectural pretensions. It was rebuilt in 1614, with a tower dating from 1710. The tower is one of the most curious in Middlesex, with two external stairways. The larger of these leads to the public gallery and the bell-tower, the smaller to a gallery known as the 'Manor House pew'. The interior is plain and un-adorned; the most conspicuous monument is a great marble affair to Lord Blythswood; but there are two seventeenth-century floor slabs concealed by carpets. The roof has great wooden tie beams and the nave a lop-sided appearance, as one side of the chancel is a foot wider than the other; while the main gallery is not horizontal. It is an odd, dark, but friendly little church.

'Scepertune' was the 'abode of shepherds' and (like other villages around it) was in the possession of St. Dunstan in 959; the ancient church on the site, as with that of Littleton, was served by the monks of Chertsey Abbey across the Thames. The rector in 1504 was William Grocyn, the great scholar of Greek, friend of John Colet, Sir Thomas More and Erasmus. Legend has it that Erasmus visited Grocyn here, and (more unlikely) that it is Erasmus's ghost that haunts the rectory. There is a long list of interesting men who were rectors here; they include John Hubbard, the hunting parson, who used hurriedly to throw his surplice over his riding kit in order to conduct a service. He was more interested in cock-fighting and prize-fighting (for which Shepperton was notorious) than in the conduct of his parish. The great John Mason Neale, was, in Victorian times, a friend and frequent guest of the rector, William Russell. Neale was reputed to speak 24 languages; he was the greatest hymnologist of the time, contributing 136 hymns to the *English Hymnal* and *Hymns ancient and modern*. Among them are *Jerusalem the golden* and *O happy band of pilgrims*. His best-known verses, however, were those to *Good King Wenceslas*. He was a prolific writer of books for the young, with a novel *Shepperton Manor*, to his credit. Neale is now only a name in a hymnbook: but two greater figures in English literature are connected with Shepperton. Thomas Love Peacock lived at Lower Halliford for 25 years until his death in 1866; he had ceased writing novels in 1831, and was, during his stay here, an examiner for the East India Company. Peacock's tomb is in the churchyard, and near the porch his daughter Margaret, who died aged three, is buried: her epitaph is four stanzas of her father's flowing Victorian verse. George Meredith, who was Peacock's son-in-law, lived at a cottage in Halliford for some years after 1851—his first book of poems was dedicated to his father-in-law. The pleasant story that George Eliot stayed at the rectory while writing *Scenes of Clerical Life* does not seem to be correct; she was living in Richmond

Riverside Towns and Villages

at the time, and her 'Shepperton' was in her native Warwickshire.

It is not surprising, however, that this district has collected a few legends. *The King's Head* is reputed to be 400 years old, and its brilliantly painted sign is a portrait of Charles II; the inevitable story that he stayed here with Nell Gwynn is perpetuated. Shepperton Square has recently been enlarged, with a lawn by the river and a few seats; a tablet records that the 'Square was handed over for the enjoyment of the people of Shepperton in April 1970'. There is a small slipway for boats, and a quiet backwater of the river, a few ducks and swans, and a good view over the water-meadows. Some half mile down the river, near Walton Bridge, is a reach of the river known as Cowey Stakes. The great palisades found there, removed well over a hundred years ago, were supposed to have been a barrier to Caesar's crossing of the Thames in 54 B.C. The archaeologists, from Camden onwards, have contradicted each other about the facts for many years.

We are here in the Old Urban District of Sunbury-on-Thames, a place that possesses two small villages, both of interest, near the great reservoir. Littleton should be reached by Littleton Lane, rather than the direct route from Shepperton, for the latter includes a hazardous ford over the River Ash. The journey is through watery fields with ballast pits here and there. Littleton is very small and has only a few houses: the vicarage, the church and the large barn-like structures of the Shepperton Film studios. The Manor House, which is within the grounds of the studios, is a spacious old house, parts of it sixteenth and seventeenth centuries. The trees alongside the river were obviously placed there by a landscape gardener; the great flower beds in the gardens are weedy and overgrown. The great house is dark and shuttered, though I was told it was 'used' by the studios; there was a fire in the house in mid-Victorian times, and evidently some rebuilding. The Wood family were originally lords of the manor; after them the Burbridges. The church, a mixture of stone and deep red brick, is on its exterior conspicuous for its red tiles—'the Middlesex trade-mark', as Nairn calls them. St. Mary Magdalene is small, but beautiful, much of it twelfth century, with a fine old roof and mediaeval stained glass. The furniture is splendid;

170

there are ancient carved choir stalls reputed to come from Winchester Cathedral. The carved screen is of the fifteenth century, the Flemish altar rails opulently carved with cherubs in the centre section. There is a Victorian window by Sir John Millais. Another circular window is dedicated to the monks of Chertsey 'who served this church 1135-1308'. High on the wall hang two small triptychs of the Italian *Trecento*. The memorials in the church are mostly Woods, in the nineteenth century all military men. One of them was at Waterloo, another in the Crimea and the Indian Mutiny. A third was a colonel in the Grenadier Guards; high in the clerestory hang 24 tattered banners of his regiment. This is a lovely little church, but a prey for vandals, the vicar told me, when I returned the keys.

On the other side of the reservoir is Charlton, a small place whose chief feature is the enormous filter beds of the Metropolitan Water Board. Robbins recorded in 1951 that it had no public transport, shops, or electricity. There has been much change in the last 20 years, and Charlton is no longer a hamlet. There are new houses, two shops, a petrol station—and electricity. Charlton's only point of interest is the *Harrow* Inn, which with its cottage adjoining is the oldest inhabited house in Middlesex—'late fifteenth or early sixteenth century', says the Royal Commission. There is indeed a thatched roof, but only the chimneys look antique; the brickwork is concealed by layers of limewash. The old lady who came to the door showed me a long room running through the house, a great black beam running across the low ceiling. She told me that when she had come to live there some 60 years ago, she was told that the house had once been a hunting lodge.

From Charlton it is a short journey to Sunbury, a discreet little town, showing few signs of modern rebuilding. Again the history goes back to 969, when the place was 'Sunnabiri' (Sunna's stronghold). It is a place of little history, and at its best down by the river, where there are a number of old houses and shops in Thames Street, near Sunbury Lock and its Ait. In one of the side streets are some good eighteenth-century houses with elegant porches. There is a quaint Victorian Inn with a Doric porch—*The Flower Pot*—its sign being the Virgin, with a lily in a flower pot beside her. Thames Street is curiously quiet—motor cars rush through, but there are few pedestrians. The large parish church of St. Mary stands near the river, with a tall tower and cupola of curious shape. The church, rebuilt in 1856 by Teulon, is according to Pevsner 'peculiarly revolting'. I was unable to test this opinion, for it is now closed, its arched windows covered with fabric. The church authorities are appealing for £85,000 to complete its repairs. The churchyard is gloomy and crowded with tombstones: just as gloomy as it was when Sykes and Oliver Twist saw it on the way to the robbery at Shepperton. The only mansion of Sunbury is the Court, an elaborate building of 1770 now used by the Salvation Army as a training centre.

CHAPTER ELEVEN

Twickenham, Teddington and the Hamptons

Nine and a half miles of the River Thames form the boundary of Twickenham, and from the 'hamm' or bend on the river the name is derived. One of the borough's historians states that the name means 'the place where two ways meet', for the River Crane joins the Thames above Twickenham. Most of this area's charm derives from its proximity to the river: indeed it must have been one of the first instances of ribbon development; houses for the nobility and gentry were being built along the river bank from early in the seventeenth century. One of its first notable residents was Francis Bacon, who in Twickenham Park found 'a place much convenient for the trial of my philosophical conclusions'. Though Bacon's house has disappeared, many of the eighteenth century residences by the Thames are still there, well preserved. Twickenham has a host of literary and historical associations: while on its border in the Hamptons are the historic Bushy Park, and a royal palace, Hampton Court.

Twentieth century Twickenham is almost purely residential: factories are few and unobtrusive: the roads are broad and there are no motorways—in fact most of the interesting parts of Twickenham may be visited along the winding road to Hampton Court which ambles pleasantly near the Thames. Away from the river there is, certainly, much very ordinary building, a good deal of it from early in this century. But the Twickenham Council showed no ambition to build multi-storey blocks of flats and the London Borough of Richmond upon Thames (into which Twickenham is now incorporated) seem equally jealous of its environment. The 'view from Richmond Hill' celebrated by so many painters, has changed, but it has not been spoiled: and from Marble Hill park, on the river, it is still possible to look out over eight miles of open space—to Ham, Richmond Park and Wimbledon Common in Surrey.

The northernmost part of the borough, St. Margaret's, is covered with Victorian villas and terrace houses: the street name Ailsa commemorates the Marquess of Ailsa, who had a house in Twickenham Park. Charles Dickens lived in Ailsa Park Villas in 1838, and left some record of his stay here: for in *Nicholas Nickleby*, he records that Miss Kenwig visits Eel Pie Island, not far away from St. Margaret's. Thackeray, Maclise, Landseer and Harrison Ainsworth all visited Ailsa Park Villas: it was one of the happier periods of Dickens' life when, he said, he had the 'grand enjoyment of idleness'. Another resident of St. Margaret's was J. M. W. Turner who lived in his self-designed Sandycombe Lodge for 12 years from 1813. His famous *View from Richmond Hill* is supposed to have been completed in the Lodge.

In St. Margaret's, too, is Twickenham's most interesting building of the twentieth century—a Roman Catholic Church named after the parish. Set apart from the main road, in a small enclave with the priest's house, this building is austere, almost uncompromising. Only a metal cross set by a square tower indicates that this grey concrete building is a church. Inside the porch is a long passage, tiled in grey, leading to an enormous wood doorway. To the left a stairway leads up to a lounge and library—a pleasant room with a wide glass wall which looks down into a great rectangular room—the 'narthex' or public space. The 'mass room' is some 50 feet wide: it rises through two storeys, its walls sheathed in blond woods. The floor is carpeted, the seats shaped like an amphitheatre, its focal point a superbly made table, the altar. There is a lectern, and the console of an electronic organ, with a simple grille set high in the wall: there is a font—a fountain—with a stoup of holy water beside it. Light comes in from two stained glass windows, completely abstract in design. This is a ceremonial theatre, and the theatrical idea persists at the end of the service. Two tall narrow doors give onto a garden: the great electrically operated doors lead into the narthex, with its seats and stools, a bar, and a coffee bar. There is a congregation of 700 here: and I was told that they enjoy this most remarkable and adventurous building.

St. Margaret's Road leads to Richmond Road: and near the junction is Marble Hill Park, with its small Palladian villa set in a corner, its lawns running down to the Thames. Marble Hill House was built for Henrietta Howard, mistress of George II. The house took a long time to build, for Roger Morris, its architect was engaged in June 1724, and the final payments were not made until the summer of 1729. Mrs. Howard was a much-frustrated woman, and was continually running out of cash. The building was a source of much speculation by Twickenham residents—among them Alexander Pope, who announced its completion prematurely, and more than once. But he was friendly to Mrs. Howard, and suggested the design of the gardens, which Bridgman subsequently laid out. After her second marriage to George Berkeley, Lady Suffolk (as she had then become) really began to enjoy her tenure of Marble Hill, and there was a constant stream of visitors, the great and the fashionable, from town. Among them was Horace Walpole, who in 1784 had started to transform his 'cottage' at Strawberry Hill: he became one of Lady Suffolk's closest friends; many of her stories of the Court were subsequently used in Walpole's writings.

Marble Hill House is charming. Its only approach to grandeur is the great room on the first floor, which rises through two storeys. It is resplendent in cream and gold, with elaborate cornices. There is a great pillared fireplace, its pediment surmounted by gilt cupids: on the walls are portraits of royalties. About this room most of the social life of the house must have revolved. Round the room there are bedrooms and retiring rooms each leading into the other. Lady Suffolk's bedroom is stately with its pillared alcove: the 'paper room' has an elaborate series of arches and decorative wallpaper. The Greater London Council, who now care for the house, are restoring, furnishing and decorating the house with immense skill. It is indeed, quite a historic villa for among the long series of tenants was another royal mistress—Mrs. Fitzherbert. There was a long period of decay from 1887 to 1901. It was only when William Cunard had acquired the whole site, with the intention of covering the park with villas, that three county councils, with the Richmond and Twickenham Councils, took action. Marble Hill park was bought, the house was preserved, and the view from Richmond Hill saved. The house was deserted on the day I visited it, and I was told that attendances had fallen off : they should not have, for Marble Hill is one of the most delightful houses in Middlesex, and its view across the Thames quite remarkable.

But Marble Hill is only the beginning of the profuse riches of this part of Twickenham. Montpelier Row, which runs alongside Marble Hill Park is full of elegant eighteenth-century houses—'one of the best examples near London of well-mannered well proportioned terrace development' writes Pevsner. A plaque on one of the houses records the residence of Alfred Lord Tennyson in 1851-52, a year after his marriage and accession to the Poet-Laureateship. South End House, nearby, is a worthy companion to the Row. Orleans House, set in a small park, remains only in the magnificent Octagon Room built by James Gibbs in 1720. This house has been restored and is open to the public. Here, in exile, lived Louis Philippe of France, from 1800 to 1814. Next door to Orleans House was the vanished Mount Lebanon, where Louis' son the Prince de Joinville, lived from 1866-71. Two other residents here were Kitty Clive, the comedienne, in Little Marble Hill : and Hannah Pritchard, great tragedienne of the age of Johnson, who created his *Irene*; she lived at Ragman's Castle. Both these houses have vanished—but never in such a half square mile of land can so many of the famous and the accomplished, the aristocratic and the notorious have lived. They include such diverse people as Thomas Fuller, Lady Diana Beauclerk, Viscountess Howe and that famous Victorian Sir John Lubbock.

Heath Lodge, not far away from here, is not particularly noticeable, but on its site stood Heath Lane Lodge, where lived one of the queerest families in Middlesex. From Heath Lane Lodge went

Laurence Shirley, fourth Earl Ferrers to his trial at Westminster, before his peers. In a fit of rage he had murdered his steward, and he was condemned to death. Horace Walpole in a series of letters written in 1760, describes it all in detail: the cool demeanour of Ferrers at his trial (though he pleaded madness)—and the solemnity of the occasion. Walpole saw the scaffold at Tyburn, hung with black crepe 'prepared by the undertakers of the family at their own expence'—he even seems to have been at Surgeon's Hall, where the body was dissected. Certainly Ferrers was no 'worthy', but he is part of the history of Muswell Hill, Acton, and Twickenham.

The quiet narrow streets close to the river have a good deal of charm, for in Lebanon Park and Sion Row there are more well-preserved houses of the eighteenth and early nineteenth century. Nowhere is this sense of the past more evident than in the stately York House, now council offices, set back in a spacious park with lawns and beds of flowers. Twickenham Council, instead of erecting an 'efficient' building of concrete, have altered and adapted this three-storey house, and have done it with taste and discretion. The chief interest of the house is its long series of tenants. The most prominent of these was Edward Hyde, Earl of Clarendon, who owned the house in 1660, lived in it for seven years, and afterwards presented it to the Duke of York, who had secretly married his daughter Anne. Count Stahrhemberg, the Viennese ambassador, lived here, adding to the amenities of the place by building a private theatre in one wing. Anne Seymour Damer, the sculptress lived here, using the house as a studio and art gallery. She was the executrix of Horace Walpole. Lord Lonsdale, a great patron of Twickenham, was a tenant; and in the eighteen sixties, the Comte de Paris joined other French exiles in Twickenham. Mountstuart Grant Duff, who succeeded the Comte, turned the place into a literary villa, and his visitors included Ernest Renan, Benjamin Jowett, Gladstone and Kinglake. The last tenant was Sir Ratan Tata the Indian merchant prince: the most obvious trace of his tenancy is the extraordinary fountain and statuary he had installed in York House gardens. Well may the Borough's guide call this a 'storied mansion'. The visitor will see little trace of antiquity save in the entrance hall, with its plaster ceiling and great carved wood fireplace; but the cinema-goer may have visited it without knowing, for it was used as a setting in *Tom Jones*.

Past York House there are more charming houses, their gardens on the river bank. Here is Twickenham Ferry, celebrated in old ballads, on an old wall there is a mark, indicating the record tide of 1774, when the river rose to eight feet above the road. A graceful little iron bridge crosses the Thames to Eel Pie Island. A good deal of river traffic is here, with river steamers moored at a landing stage: there is a larger boat house with much coming and going of eights and skiffs. Eel Pie Island looks untidy, with a conglomeration of small houses and bungalows: it has a tea garden and somewhere, I was told, a bird sanctuary. But the island is not what it was—the Eel Pie Hotel, once a favourite resort of Londoners, is in a state of decay, its licence lost some time ago. Its large and very noisy jazz festivals brought no pleasure to the local inhabitants, and the hotel is now occupied by a hippy community. So the island remains unplanned: like the lampreys for which the place was famous in the eighteenth century, the eels and the pies have vanished.

A sloping lane leads from the river up to the High Street, passing Dial House, a charming vicarage. The name Arragon on another house is a reminder that Katherine of Aragon stayed in Twickenham while awaiting her divorce from Henry VIII: but it was not here, but in the old Manor House not far away. In the high street, called King Street, stands the parish church of St. Mary: its old tower is fifteenth century, the body of the church rebuilt by John James in 1714-15. Pevsner praises its magnificent brickwork and its fine Tuscan pilasters—but he was disappointed by the interior. He could not have seen it at its best. I found it exhilarating after the Gothic gloom of many Middlesex churches: resplendent in cream and gold, with its fine woodwork gleaming after a recent redecoration, its chief feature is the two galleries with a remarkable series of ornate monuments. The earliest is that of Francis Poulton (1642) its two figures holding a skull, 'erected and composed by teares, by the pensive son and daughter'. The whole series of tombs is an anthology of English monumental sculpture, for Bird, Bushnell, Scheemakers,

178

Rysbrack and the younger John Bacon are all represented. There are two monuments to Alexander Pope—one of them an obelisk, with a plaque bearing the inscription

'Heroes and kings your distance keep
In peace let one poor poet sleep
Who never flattered folks like you
Let Horace blush, and Virgil too'

There is a monument to Pope's parents in the church : and one, outside, to Mary Beach, his nurse; while the poet himself composed the couplets on the tomb of Nathaniel Piggott. The spirit of the Augustan age seems to pervade this church, and when I visited it my enjoyment was enhanced by an orchestra which assembled in the nave and proceeded to play a stately overture by Telemann : very much in keeping with the atmosphere. From St. Mary's I went in search of Alexander Pope.

'Pope's Villa' in Cross Deep is so named : but this rambling Victorian mansion is the third house on the site, and is now the St. Catherine's Convent School for Girls. Alexander Pope leased a small house with five acres of ground in 1719, and promptly began to enlarge the house and embellish the grounds. 'Eighteenth-century England was the paradise of the amateur' wrote Kenneth Clark 'and these eighteenth-century amateurs were the inheritors of the Renaissance idea of universal man'. Pope was just such an amateur—philosopher, architect and landscape-gardener : and here, until his death in 1744 he wrote, improved the building, cultivated his garden, received his friends and discoursed philosophy. A small lawn lay in front of the villa, bordering the Thames : on it he planted a weeping willow, the first to be seen in England. The main garden was across the road to Hampton Court. There he laid out the beds, planted trees and shrubs, cultivated his 'hartichokes' and embellished with urns and obelisks. Connecting the two gardens was his underground grotto : the grotto survives, and I was permitted to see it by permission of the Mother in charge of the convent. It is a gloomy cold place, some nine feet high, lined with slabs of rock, very solidly

179

built, for it survived a bomb during the Second World War. Here and there in the ceiling are patches of shells, flints and rock crystals: there are still two fragments of the old mirrors in one corner. The mirrors reflected the light from a central lamp so that 'a thousand pointed rays glitter': here Pope wrote his satires and epistles, the *Essay on Man* and *The Dunciad*. Here he sat with his friends, talking, admiring the view of the Thames through the arch of the tunnel. The urns that decorated the entrance have gone away for restoration: one obelisk survives in a house across the road: the incised stones of the *Arma Christi* are still above the arch of the tunnel. There is not much left: but one can still feel the peace and solitude of the vanished villa—the 'glory of my little kingdom' as Pope called it. The poet can still afford the modern man some inspiration: Andrzev Panufnik, the Polish composer who lives on the Thames within sight of the villa has recently set Pope's *Universal Prayer* to music.

Close to Cross Deep lies Twickenham's main shopping centre, busy, noisy, a patchwork of various styles. But the Green, once the centre of the village, has a few old houses and some literary associations. Henry Fielding lived here in 1784, before his final removal to Ealing. In the now vanished Saville House lived Lady Mary Wortley Montague, near her friend Pope. The Green lies on the Staines Road; through the shopping centre and along Whitton Road lies the most recently developed part of Twickenham, north of the Chertsey Road, the district's only arterial road. The housing, consisting of modern semidetached villas, is unremarkable: but the church built to serve the estate is unusual, for its tower is of the seventeenth century, the church twentieth century. All Hallows tower is Wren's tower from the City of London church of that name, transported stone by stone and re-erected after demolition in 1938. The tower has been linked by a cloister to the 1940 church, designed by Robert Atkinson. Its interior is lofty, with great arches and a fine coffered roof; the grey austerity of the place forms a fine setting for Wren's magnificent woodwork of 1694, which was brought here with the tower. The altar, pulpit, choir and churchwardens' stalls are splendidly carved and richly gilt, all of them having been carefully restored by a Twickenham craftsman. The original organ of 1708 has also been restored and rebuilt in its fine old case—and everything is seen to the best advantage in its austere modern setting. The oldest monuments have been transferred from the city church and now line the cloister, the finest of them being that of Edward Tyson, the surgeon. In the tower hangs a grand carved Royal Arms, one of the most remarkable in Britain: above it in the bell-loft are the ten bells of the old city church. The church, and a small square containing the vicarage are close to the hurrying traffic of the arterial road.

Whitton, before 1935 a district of market-gardens, contains one place which to thousands of people is 'Twickenham'—the Rugby Union Football Club where many international matches are played. It is in no way remarkable: a quadrangle of green turf surrounded by stands and vast car-parks, only coming to life when matches are played. Then it is a place of pilgrimage: its vast crowds produce the famous 'Twickenham roar'—and the end of play brings traffic jams through half Middlesex. There are three parks in this area: the largest of them (though not a public park) contains Kneller Hall, once the mansion of Sir Godfrey Kneller. He was a man of some importance, having painted the portraits of ten Kings: he was important in Twickenham, becoming a churchwarden and a Justice of the Peace. He had quarrels with Pope: they continued even after Kneller's death, for his widow wanted the most important site in the church for her husband's monuments—and Pope's father was buried there. So there is no monument to Sir Godfrey in Twickenham church. The hall has been much altered since 1723 when the owner died, and only the front of the house has any architectural vigour left: it is now the Royal Military School of Music. Here the Army's musicians are trained, 400 of them at a time, on a year's course. The Hall is not, generally, open to the public, and when I visited it, a young Guardsman was delegated to show me round. I was told that much of the original decorations have vanished, including Landscroon's Murals, though some of the original panelling is retained in the Adjutant's quarters, and there is a small museum. The School is run on strictly military lines, with reveille being blown by one of the trumpeters—the trumpeters of Kneller Hall are famous: they have played at Coronations, and even occasionally at performances of *Aïda*. Not only brass players, but all varieties of musicians are trained here: there are quartets, string orchestras and a dance band. The grounds contain a neat terrace of bungalows for the instructors and a fine open-air arena, where concerts are held in the summer months. There are, I was told, half a million pounds' worth of musical instruments in the building—this alone justifies the military precautions. As I left I noticed a neat touch—the great brass name plate of the Great Western Railway locomotive 'Kneller Hall' is fixed to the railings at the gate.

Murray Park, close to the Hall, is now simply an open space with some fine trees: but two interesting houses once stood here. The first was the residence of Archibald Duke of Argyll—he was important enough to obtain a grant of a portion of Hounslow Heath to enlarge his demesne: and in the grounds he planted cedars, Scotch firs and exotic trees. Walpole praised him for these innovations, which 'contributed essentially to the richness of modern landscape'. Whether any of the trees in the park are Argyll's, I could not discover. The Argyll residence was subsequently sold to Sir William Chambers who converted it into a Palladian villa, and the grounds were filled with statues, ruins and temples. All these have now disappeared, and with them the great collections formed by Chambers. Whitton's second park, Kneller Gardens, is municipalised, but has some charm, for the River Crane flows through it, visible for the first time after many miles of its course: and here it meets the artificial stream of the Duke of Northumberland's river.

Whitton's neighbouring parish, Fulwell, has few attractions except two golf courses. Near the Staines Road in a tiny cottage lived a curious character: Joanna Southcott, whose fanatical prophesies terrified many of the simple-minded from 1792 onwards. She died in Fulwell in 1814, but her legend lingers on in occasional advertisements in the press, warning of ruin when her 'secret box' is opened. It was opened in 1927 by a bishop and was 'found to contain nothing of interest'. Where the box is now no one can say.

It is necessary to go back towards the river to find the house of Twickenham's most fascinating character—Horace Walpole—at

Strawberry Hill. It is set back from Waldegrave Road, behind a small courtyard: and here is Walpole's 'fantastic fabric'. It is a miniature Gothic castle in golden stucco, battlemented, turreted, with lancet windows: the entrance abounds in shields and ornaments. The building is now part of a larger complex, St. Mary's Training College, a Catholic community, and visits are permitted by previous arrangement. I visited the house at a holiday period, and was, very graciously, allowed to examine its pleasures alone, my only guide the invaluable volume of Pevsner. And pleasures they are: the first impressions were of gaiety, in the sunny little parlour with its golden flock-paper, and the elaborately decorated hall staircase, with its pink wallpaper ornamented with gothic fretwork. The balusters on the staircase are delicate, the newel posts each surmounted by a tiny gilt antelope holding a blue shield with Walpole's monogram: he loved this shield and monogram—they are all over the house. The first floor landing leading to the principal rooms has charming arches in blue, decorated with gilt *fleurs de lis*: above the staircase is a roof-lantern glowing with coloured glass. The hall is in fact just as Horace Walpole described it in a letter 'so pretty and so small that I am inclined to wrap it up and send it to you'. Each room has its pleasures. The library has exuberant gothic bookcases, copied from a screen in old St. Paul's, a great chimneypiece and an elaborate plaster ceiling: its great windows look over green lawns. There is a great bedchamber with the bed behind a gothic screen: there is the 'Holbein room' with its fine ceiling. There is an abundance of painted glass in the window mouldings—Walpole collected glass from half Europe, for there are fragments from France, Italy and the Netherlands, all with seventeenth-century dates. The climax is the gallery, with a fan vaulted ceiling copied from the Henry VII chapel in Westminster, all in cream plaster, elaborately gilt with a profusion of mirrors to add to the gaiety.

Walpole employed four architects to carry out his ideas: and looking around Strawberry Hill, one cannot but feel the same pleasure as the owner did in his 'filigree box ... a romance in lath and plaster'—for this is a home, not a palace like Syon or Osterley. Here he wrote his innumerable letters, his historical memoirs, that extraordinary Gothic novel, *The Castle of Otranto*; here he established the Strawberry Hill Press. He collected many things, and was always willing to show them, even printing tickets of admission. In this house he entertained many of his friends. His neighbours included Kitty Clive, to whom he gave the lease of Little Strawberry Hill, and the two charming Misses Berry, one of them becoming his literary executor. He was a remarkable man : and his house was also remarkable. As Pevsner writes 'by far the most important and rewarding of all the monuments of Twickenham'. Horace Walpole himself is delineated by Guy Chapman, who wrote that he 'was at the centre of the world of his day, and summed it up with affectionate amusement'.

Strawberry Hill is in Teddington, a village that grew rapidly into a middle-class suburb after the First World War. There are still parts of the village left down by the river, where Teddington Lock marks the boundary between the tidal and non-tidal Thames. There is always some activity near the bridge across the Thames, with boats being slipped into the water, a line of placid fishermen along the bank, and much coming and going from Tough's Shipyard. There are two pleasant looking inns : the most prominent building is the long low brick and glass studio of Thames Television. There is some industry in Teddington, but it is chiefly represented by research laboratories—for the Admiralty, for paint and chemicals; and there is one that is famous—the National Physical Laboratory.

The High Street is rather sleepy, for there is little through traffic : and here there are two parish churches on opposite sides of a street. The larger, St. Alban, replaced the old church, and was grandiosely named the Cathedral of the Thames Valley. It remains incomplete, only the tremendous nave having been built. The smaller church, St. Mary, dates from 1750, but has been much altered. It is a sad looking little place, its graveyard overgrown and untended. But here, as usual, the village worthies are to be found. The chief monument in the church is to Sir Orlando Bridgeman, who was commissioner to Charles I at the Treaty of Uxbridge : the monument of 1674, together with a sixteenth century brass, are relics of an earlier foundation. The vicar of the church for 50 years was Stephen Hales :

he carried on a dual career, for he made notable researches in physics, was a Fellow of the Royal Society, and an eighteenth-century authority on ventilation. The tablet to 'Margaret Woffington, spinster' is to the famous Peg Woffington, who played Polly Peachum in *The Beggar's Opera*. Her cottage nearby, which legend says she intended to be almshouses, are anything but: one of them is a tea-shop. Thomas Traherne the metaphysical poet was curate of Teddington for two years, and is buried here. John Walter, founder of *The Times* lived in Teddington and died there in 1819. Lastly there is Richard Doddridge Blackmore, who worshipped at the church, and lived in Teddington from 1858 to 1900 at Gomer House. *Lorna Doone* and 14 other novels were written there: and a plaque records his residence. Alexander Herzen, Russia's greatest diarist, lived in Elmfield House, a fine eighteenth-century mansion, in 1863-4: and William Penn lived in Teddington for a year, though nobody knows where. This, indeed, is a formidable list of worthies for this twentieth-century suburb: the most famous name of this century—Sir Noel Coward—is not yet commemorated.

Lower down the river Thames are the last two of Twickenham's villages, Hampton and Hampton Wick. Hampton itself is on the border with Sunbury: and away from the vast grey buildings of the Metropolitan Water Board, in Thames Street, Church Street and High Street are the remains of an eighteenth-century village. The High Street is quiet, with little through traffic and few shops: old buildings and new mingle pleasantly. The earlier houses are well cared for. Among them is the eighteenth-century Grove House, preserved by an electronics firm and the Old Grange of 1630, with its charming curved gables. Orme House, elegantly restored, is labelled 1698, and was once the residence of Thomas Holloway, engraver to George III. 'Penn's House', very much restored is allegedly the home of Sibel Penn, nurse to Edward VI: the stained glass window visible from the street is evidently her portrait. The *Red Lion* at the corner is a modern hotel, but is built on the site of a sixteenth-century hunting lodge which Henry VIII is reputed to have used. Farther along the riverside is a larger house, St. Alban's, said to have been built for Nell Gwynne. So Hampton has historical connections with six centuries.

The centre of all this is St. Mary's Church, standing on the riverside, a disappointing piece of Victorian gothic of the eighteen thirties: but its records go back to 1342, and many of its old monuments have been preserved. The first to be seen is the recumbent effigy of Sibel Penn, placed, rather awkwardly, in a niche in the vestibule: she has a long rhyming epitaph. Within the body of the church there are inscriptions and monuments to many of Hampton's worthies—one of the earliest is to Edmund Pigeon, Yeoman of the Jewel-House to Henry VIII, and Clerk of the Robes to Queen Elizabeth. There are three eighteenth-century worthies: Thomas Rosomon, owner of Sadler's Wells theatre: John Beard the tenor; and David Garrick, the great actor's nephew. Some of the tombs are curiously touching: for instance those of Captain A. Ellick, comptroller general of the Coastguards, with a coastguard mourning by his coffin and of Huntington Shaw, master-worker in wrought-iron, laconically said to be 'an artist in his way'. The most ornate tomb is that of Susanna Thomas, who with her arm reclining on an urn, sits reading to her mother. Pevsner calls it a 'noble composition': the insensitive Harris in *Three Men in a Boat* calls it a 'funny tomb'. There are two interesting modern stained glass windows designed by Eric Fraser, who lives in the village. The most controversial object is a large mural on the wall: beneath the figure of Christ in Glory are assembled the figures of dozens of people associated with the Hamptons: Henry VIII, Sibel Penn, Wolsey—down the centuries to the congregation of 1952. St. Mary's Church, unprepossessing at first, is fascinating once one has entered it.

Coming from the front porch we are on the riverside. The view down the Thames towards Taggs Island is charming. Just past the cross-roads and some few feet below road level is Garrick's Lawn. Its domed classic temple, placed there by Garrick, contains Roubiliac's statue of Shakespeare, for which the great actor sat as a model. Here on the lawn the public is allowed to picnic, just as David Garrick and his friends did. There are two elegant conversation pieces by Zoffany of this scene: in one David Garrick and his wife stand, nicely posed on the steps of the temple, a small boy playing behind its pillars : their great hound lies on the lawn, while a footman approaches with a tea-tray. In the other piece, the Garricks and their friends are grouped in conversation round the tea table, while George Garrick is fishing.

Across the road from the lawn is Garrick's villa, Hampton House, redesigned and ornamented by Robert Adam in 1755. The villa is perhaps not in Adam's best manner : Pevsner calls it 'aesthetically unsatisfying' : there was some skimping, maybe, for the pillars are of wood rather than stone; they have suffered a little during 200 years, for they are now bound up with iron bands. But this is a pleasant looking villa today, well maintained, though now turned into flats. This was Garrick's domain from 1757, when he was at the height of his fame. Here he entertained his friends to dinners, garden parties and evening fêtes, with coloured lamps hung all over the grounds. Even Horace Walpole, who was particular about such matters, thought the company was good : '*sur assez bon ton* for a player'. The main hall of the villa is pleasant, but not as spacious as it must have been : one of the residents whom I met there told me that much of the original woodwork and the fine fireplaces have been preserved. I was allowed, too, to go round to the lawn and there to catch a glimpse of the fine 'Bow Room', which Garrick used as a library. Here Samuel Johnson, on one of his visits, tore David's books in their fine bindings from the shelves : after a glance at them, throwing them on the floor; and when Garrick protested muttered 'Lookee David, you do understand plays, but know nothing about books!'. The tunnel which connects the back lawn with that on the river is still preserved—the 'grotto-arch' through which Garrick drove a golf-ball into the Thames after one of his famous parties.

This part of Hampton Village is still one of the pleasantest spots on the Thames, and one can imagine how peaceful a place it was when Garrick lived there. Down river is Tagg's Island, a place that has undergone many vicissitudes, since 80 years ago when the gypsies who occupied it were expelled, and laid a curse on it. The island has always been devoted to entertainment. Its most famous building the 'Karsino', a combination of hotel, dance-hall, restaurant and theatre of varieties, has recently been demolished. It belonged to the famous Fred Karno, who schooled such comedians as Charles Chaplin, Stan Laurel and Will Hay : many of 'Fred Karno's Boys' played here before he went bankrupt in 1927.

It would have been pleasant to approach Hampton Wick along the river. But I had to go by road : and the road from Teddington is one of the few in the old borough of Twickenham where planning and preservation have been absent. 'Wic' means a dairy farm, but all traces of farming have now gone. Hampton Wick, once the smallest of urban districts in Middlesex, is redeemed by its open spaces. They are Bushy Park and Hampton Court Park. Bushy Park is over 1,100 acres in extent : Hampton Court Park almost as large as Hyde Park and Kensington Gardens together, and its palace and gardens make it the most historic site in Middlesex.

Bushy Park is celebrated for its triple avenue of chestnuts and limes, over a mile long, which runs through the park from Hampton Court to Sandy Lane. In May, when the chestnuts are in flower the avenue is one of the sights of the county, and at weekends the park is crowded with thousands of visitors. The view straight down the avenue is one of great splendour, though a little spoilt at one end by building. The great avenue is said to have been planted on the instructions of William III; William IV lived in a house in the park for 38 years, in the guise of a gentleman-farmer. Still remembered by a memorial plaque in Sandy Lane is Timothy Bennett, the worthy shoemaker of Hampton Wick who in 1752, at the age of 75, sued the Ranger of the park and 'by a vigorous application of the laws of his country, obtained a free passage through Bushy Park'. The Lodge, once the Ranger's house, is now part of the National Physical Laboratory. There is a fine fountain of Diana some way up the chestnut avenue, there are artificial waters, and two small lakes; while herds of deer roam around. Like Osterley, Bushy underwent a transformation during the Second World War, for the park, from 1941-45 was one of the quarters for the American Expeditionary Forces in Europe. The ground was strewn with army huts, the lakes covered with camouflage nets. General Eisenhower was a frequent visitor, the great Joe Louis boxed in an open-air arena for the entertainment of the troops. The ladies of Hampton, Teddington and nearby Kingston staffed the American Red Cross Club, and worked the telephone switchboard. So the history of Bushy Park covers a number of centuries. Richard Steele, who frequently stayed in the lodge, dedicated a volume of *The Tatler* to Lord Halifax, the ranger, in 1711. He wrote of 'the elegant solitude of this place and the greatest pleasures of it'. Early on a May morning, before the crowds have arrived, with the chestnuts in flower, the twentieth-century visitor may feel much the same.

The best old houses of Hampton Wick are to be found round the entrances to Bushy Park and Hampton Court. Both parks are maintained by the Crown, and in and around them were gathered the residences of many people connected with the court; there are still a number of 'grace and favour' residences within the palace precincts. Hampton Green is very spacious, with a number of fine eighteenth-century houses. They include Old Court House where Christopher Wren lived. Hampton Court Bridge is one of Sir Edward Lutyens' best designs. There is a continuous coming and going at most times of the year on Hampton Green: in the summer coach after coach discharges its load of tourists, and the car-parks seem always to be full.

Hampton Court is, surely, the climax of the fine buildings of Middlesex. Day after day may be spent exploring it: the Royal Commission devotes 20 pages to listing its monuments, Pevsner an equal number. It is a palace full of history, from 1514, when the manor was bought by Thomas Wolsey from the Hospitallers of St. John. He then started to build the largest palace in England. In 1526, he presented it to Henry VIII who is reputed to have spent more on it than any other of his palaces. Elizabeth I delighted in the palace and its gardens. James I gave great entertainments here: Charles I here spent his honeymoon. During the 'troubles' Charles was kept under restraint in the palace where John Evelyn visited him. It was one of Oliver Cromwell's residences. It was a favourite residence of William III, and it was in Hampton Court Park that he had the riding accident that subsequently led to his death. George II was the last monarch to live here. The royal, the noble, the great and the privileged have enjoyed Hampton Court through the centuries. On the accession of Queen Victoria in 1837, the palace was finally opened to the public.

The palace is vast, diverse, with something of interest for everyone: its gardens are full of flowers from spring onwards, its halls and courts echo with the steps of thousands of tourists. The fountains in the main avenue, fed by waters of the Longford river, are splendid to look on. For the gardener there is the Orangery and the Great Vine, the sunken Italian garden, the splendid herbaceous borders. The Privy Garden has the great wrought-iron screen designed by Tijou and made by Huntingdon Shaw of Hampton. Successive epochs of English architecture are to be seen, the most magnificent being the two great courts designed by Christopher Wren. Collections of armour and tapestries, royal portraits without number, frescoes and ceiling paintings are here; the most spectacular, the great series of cartoons by Mantegna, purchased by Charles I from the Gonzaga family.

The whole of the south front of the palace has recently undergone a tremendous four-year restoration by craftsmen of the Ministry of Works. Window frames and stone ornaments have been copied and replaced: modern bricks have been 'rubbed down' to Tudor sizes. Many discoveries have been made including the initials of seventeenth-century workmen carved on the wood and stone of the King's Staircase. There was also a Wren curtain brick wall, 60 feet high, which was unkeyed to the Tudor wall behind it. There is more restoration to be done in other parts of the building. The process is continuous: the 300 feet long front, however, now looks magnificent. Half a million people visit Hampton Court every year: the palace is part of our national, rather the county's, heritage. It is, however, the best place to end a tour of Twickenham—and of Middlesex.

Index

Index

Index

Ibbetson, Julius Caesar, 89
Ickenham, 118-21
Inns and public houses, 29, 33, 35, 39, 41, 44, 46, 47, 49, 50, 55, 59, 62, 70, 74, 78, 88, 89, 97, 132, 134, 142, 145, 146, 152, 160, 163, 170, 171, 187
Ironside, Edmond, 149
Isleworth, 138, 152-3

Jackson, Holbrook, 62
James I, 33, 191
James, John, 66
Jebb, Richard, 34
Jellicoe, G. A., 96
Jersey, Earls of, 154
John, King, 163
Johnson, John, 62
Johnson, Samuel, 43, 102, 176, 189
Joinville, Francois d'Orleans, Prince, 176
Jones, Inigo, 32, 141, 164
Jonson, Ben, 136
Julius Caesar, 149, 170

Karno, Fred, 190
Katherine of Aragon, 178
Kaufmann, Angelica, 63
Keats, John, 27-8, 35, 44
Kelly, Frances Maria, 159-60
Kendal, Melusina, Duchess, 152
Kensal Rise, 89
Kent, Edward, Duke, 105
Kent, William, 34, 140, 141, 143
Ken Wood House, 47
Kenyon, A. W., 81
Kilburn, 87, 89-90
Kinge, Alexander, 48
'King John's Palace', 163
Kingsbury, 67-9, 77
King's College, Cambridge, 110, 118
Kingsley, Henry and Mary, 44
Kneller Hall, 180-81
Kneller, Sir Godfrey, 181
Knyvett, Thomas, Lord, 161-2
Kodak, Ltd., 73

Laguerre, Louis, 66
Laleham, 164, 167
Lamb, Charles, 27-8, 31, 73, 159
Lanfranc, Archbishop, 72
Langley, William, 157, 161
Lanscroon, 36, 181
Laundries, 87
Lawes, Henry, 136
Lawrence, Sir George, 103
Lawrence, Sir Henry, 103
Lawrence, Sir John, 35
Lea Navigation, 25, 29, 30
Lea, river, 14, 20, 23, 25, 26, 29, 30
Lea Valley Development, 26
Lehmann, Frederick, 43

Lehmann, Liza, 77
Libraries, 42, 48, 83, 85, 97, 103-4, 118, 119, 153
Linnaeus, Carl, 61
Littleberries, 60
Littleton, 170
Livingstone, David, 51
London, 14, 15, 89
London Boroughs Act, 15
London Natural History Society, 83
London Postal Region, 120, 121
London Stone, 164
London Transport, 15, 25
Longford river, 122, 163, 192
Longmore, Edward, 60
Lonsdale, H. C. Lowther, Earl, 177
Loudon, John Claudius, 74, 101
Louis, Joe, 190
Louis-Philippe, 103, 176
Loutherbourg, Philip de, 143
Lubbock, Sir John, 176
Lucan, Charles Bingham, Earl, 167
Lutyens, Sir Edwyn, 54, 55, 191
Lyon, John, 70, 72, 84

Mansfield, William Murray, Earl, 47
Manor House, Southall, 130
Mantegna, Andrea, 192
Marble Hill House, 174, 175-6 : 148
Marryat, Frederick, 35, 103
Marston, John, 136
Marvell, Andrew, 45
Masefield, Sir John, 45
Maufe, Edward, 96, 106
Mazzini, Giuseppe, 42
Mee, Arthur, ix
Mendelssohn-Bartholdy, Felix, 124
Meredith, George, 169
Metropolitan Water Board, 171, 187
Middlesex County Council, 15, 41, 50, 81, 118, 126, 140, 144
Middlesex Cricket Club, 16
Middlesex Guildhall, 16
Middlesex Regiment, 15-16
Middlesex Society, 123
Millais, Sir John, 171
Miller, Joe, 145
Millet family, 108
Mill Hill, 60-62
Mill Hill School, 61 : 39
Milman, H. H., 77
Milton, John, 136
Minto, Gilbert, Earl, 49
Monk, George, Duke of Albemarle, 49
Montague, Lady Mary Wortley, 180
Montez, Lola, 97
Moore, Temple, 59
Moore, Thomas, 42, 50
Morier, Sir Robert, 116
Morland, George, 46

197

Index

Rothschild family, 100-101
Roubiliac, Louis F., 188
Roundwood Park, 90
Rous, Francis, 92
Roy, William, 158
Royal Air Force, 63, 113, 133
Royal Commission on Historical Monuments, viii, 34, 52, 116, 163, 171, 191
Royal Small Arms Factory, 30
Rugby Union Football Club, 181
Ruislip, 117-18
Runnymede, 163
Russell, Lord William, 62
Rye House Plot, 62
Ryland, W. W., 159
Rysbrack, Michael, 135, 179

Sadler, F., 101
St. Bernard's Hospital, 106
St. John Hospitallers, 50, 134
St. Margaret's, 174-5
Salvation Army, 172
Sambrooke, Sir S., 51
Sassoon, Sir Edward, 34
Savundra, Emil, 47
Sawyer, Elizabeth, 27
Say family, 119
Scarburgh, Sir Charles, 124
Scheemakers, Pieter, 179
Scott, Sir Gilbert, 71, 117
Scott, Giles Gilbert, 91, 106, 127
Scott, Sir Walter, 34, 79
Sedley, Sir Charles, 136
Segontiacum, 164
Selbourne Society, 109
Seymour, Laura, 88
Shaftesbury, A. A. Cooper, Earl, 71
Shakespeare, William, 136
Sharpe, Sir Montagu, ix, 107, 109
Shaw, Huntingdon, 188, 192
Shaw, Norman, 78, 97
Shelley, Percy Bysshe, 152
Sheppard, Jack, 49, 90
Shepperton, 168-70
Shepperton Film Studios, 170
Sherborne family, 160
Sheridan, R. B., 70, 71, 152
Shoreditch family, 119
Shovell, Sir Cloudesley, 117
Sipson, 127
Skan Ogle, 110
Skippon, Philip, 92, 95
Smeaton, John, 25
Smirke, Sydney, 101
Soane, Sir John, 79, 103
Somerset, Sir Alfred, 32
Somerset, Edward Seymour, Duke, 150
Southall, 155
Southcott, Joanna, 182
Southgate, 31, 35, 36, 37

South Mimms, 52
Spenser, Edmund, 136
Sprignell, Richard, 45
Squire, William Barclay, 159
Stahrhemberg, Ernst Rüdiger, Count, 177
Staines, 15, 163-4
Stanmore, 65, 80-81
Stanwell, 161
Steele, Richard, 191
Stephens, H. C., 49
Stone, Nicholas, 124, 162
Stone, Reynolds, 45
Strand-on-the-Green, 144-5 : 94
Strawberry Hill House, 158, 185-6 : 147
Streater, Robert, 120
Stroud Green, 38
Sudbury, 85-6
Sulloniacae, 64
Sunbury, 15, 170, 171-2
Sunbury Court, 172 : 58
Surrey, 15, 20, 138, 160, 174
Swakelys House, 119, 120-21 : 58
Syon House and Park, 138, 150-51 : 111
and 112

Tagg's Island, 188, 189-90
Tarleton family, 135
Tata, Sir Ratan, 177
Taverner, Richard, 102
Taylor, Sir William, 136
Technicolor, Ltd., 128
Tecton and Lubetkin, 46
Teddington, 186-7
Tegetmeier, W. B., 43
Telford, Thomas, 25, 45
Tennyson, Alfred, Lord, 176
Teulon, S. S., 102, 116, 172
Thackeray, William Makepeace, 103, 142, 174
Thames, river, 13, 14, 82, 138, 142, 144, 145, 149, 164, 167-73 *passim*, 175, 177, 178, 180, 182, 186
Thamesis Street, 13
Thomas, Susanna, 188
Thorne, James, ix
Thornhill, Sir James, 36, 143
Thornycroft, Sir John, 142
Thorp, Nicholas, 162
Three men in a boat, 188
Tiepolo, Giambattista, 59
Tiercelin, Joseph, 132
Tijou, Jean, 192
Tijou Screen, *183*
Tilbury, Mr., 77
Tiptoft, Lady Joyce, 31
Tom Jones, 178
Tooke, John Horne, 102
Tottenham, 16, 23-6
Tottenham Hotspur, 25
Town Halls, 19, 42, 50, 59, 83, 157

199